TAIT COLES

CRITICAL PEDAGOGY

A TEACHER'S COMPANION

JOHN CATT
FROM HODDER EDUCATION

Orders: please contact Hachette UK Distribution, Hely Hutchinson Centre, Milton Road, Didcot, Oxfordshire, OX11 7HH. Telephone: +44 (0)1235 827827. Email education@hachette.co.uk. Lines are open from 9 a.m. to 5 p.m., Monday to Friday.

ISBN: 9781398388642

© Tait Coles 2024

First published in 2024 by
John Catt from Hodder Education,
An Hachette UK Company
15 Riduna Park, Station Road,
Melton, Woodbridge IP12 1QT
Telephone: +44 (0)1394 389850
www.johncatt.com

A catalogue record for this title is available from the British Library

MIX
Paper | Supporting
responsible forestry
FSC
www.fsc.org
FSC™ C104740

PRAISE FOR CRITICAL PEDAGOGY
A TEACHER'S COMPANION

Critical Pedagogy: a teacher's companion is one of the best books written on the meaning, purpose and use of critical pedagogy in the classroom in the last few decades. Not only is it beautifully written, while being rigorous and accessible, but it also covers a wide area of crucial concerns regarding what critical pedagogy is and is not, especially in light of the myths and falsehoods used to attack it. Moreover, it is more than a defence and articulation regarding critical pedagogy – it is a text that every educator should read in order to evaluate and rethink their own classroom visions and practices as part of a broader practice of freedom and empowerment. This is a brilliant book and is sorely needed at a time when all levels of education are under attack by extremist groups. Education and critical pedagogy are crucial in a democracy and this book makes that case with a clarity, urgency and passion that is much needed.

Henry A. Giroux, Chair for Scholarship in the Public Interest and Paulo Freire Distinguished Scholar in Critical Pedagogy, McMaster University, Canada

Critical Pedagogy: a teacher's companion is a thorough, robust and timely argument for the need for criticality in teaching, to empower students and teachers alike. Educators will undoubtedly benefit from this book. We need to engage with politics, history, academia and core values and this book offers vital guidance in all these areas.

Jeffrey Boakye, author, educator, speaker, broadcaster and journalist

Tait Coles' *Critical Pedagogy: a teacher's companion* is essential reading for those new to the teaching profession, and a compelling and illuminating guide for educators eager to revolutionise their teaching practices. The book offers hope for teachers who believe in the power of education to be a transformative force, while fostering a deeper understanding of social justice and equity. The strength of the book lies in its ability to blend theory with practical strategies, making it accessible for educators at all levels. Coles skilfully unpacks the foundational principles of critical pedagogy, demonstrating how they can be applied in diverse classroom settings. Throughout the book there is an emphasis on cultivating a reflective and inclusive approach to education. Coles invites educators to commit to critically examine their own assumptions, biases and practices. This self-reflective approach serves as a powerful catalyst for personal and professional growth, encouraging teachers to create inclusive learning environments in their schools and colleges. A must-read for educators who aspire to go beyond traditional teaching paradigms and embark on a journey of transformative education. Coles has crafted a seminal work that both informs and inspires, leaving readers with a renewed sense of purpose and the tools to effect positive change in their classrooms and communities.

Dr Sadia Habib, lecturer in education, University of Manchester

Tait Coles' *Critical Pedagogy: a teacher's companion* is a real game-changer for anyone in education. It's like a deep dive into how we can make our classrooms more empowering and fair, especially for those students who often get overlooked. Coles doesn't just stick to the old ways of teaching; he challenges us to think differently and use education to fight against social injustice. It's a must-read if you're into teaching that goes beyond the textbooks and really makes a difference. In an age of compliance and conformity, education needs anger and fury to challenge the preconceived ideas that too many have accepted.

Matt Perry, headteacher, Halifax Academy

Tait Coles' *Critical Pedagogy: a teacher's companion* is an invaluable source for anyone involved or interested in adopting a rights-based perspective when thinking about their teaching practice. The narrative is engaging, absorbing and accessible, and the text rattles along at a pace that feels comfortable and authentic. The book provides the perfect opportunity to take stock of where we are as a profession. More importantly, it suggests that we are in control of our future destiny and that we as practitioners can strengthen the idea of rights-led practice if we value the contribution of the young people we support. Coles asks some very difficult questions of the reader, but the result is a text that is robust in its assertions and sound in terms of ideology and philosophy. I can't stress enough how important this book is and how timely it feels.

Brian Mitchell, School of Social Sciences, University of Bradford

Critical Pedagogy: a teacher's companion is a refreshing, wide-ranging read with references locally and internationally that takes a practical and inspiring approach to critical pedagogy.

**Evie Manning, co-artistic director, Common Wealth/
Speakers Corner, Bradford**

In this book, Tait Coles sets out a compelling and convincing argument for the centring of critical pedagogy within schools. Through a robust critique of authoritarian and damaging contemporary pedagogical practice, we understand how schooling is currently centred around economic imperatives at the expense of creativity, care and vital reimaginings of a better world. A series of thought-provoking chapters, which disrupt normative ideas of neutrality and meritocracy, offer the opportunity for teachers to explore key issues of power, agency and oppression. Such inquiry is vital in times of instrumentalism and transmissive approaches to both teaching and teacher education, which deny the chance to ask the bigger philosophical and values-based questions. As such, this book would lend itself to group readings and activities by teacher collectives who wish to disrupt and reimagine 'education as usual'. This book is also recommended for anyone (in education or wider community contexts) wanting to understand what critical pedagogy is, and how it can be used for good in our existing and future educational systems.

Dr Kay Sidebottom, lecturer in education, University of Stirling

Critical Pedagogy: a teacher's companion exceeds expectations of being transformative and refreshing. The purpose of this book is clear: a tool for educators promoting the significance of having honest and powerful dialogues within a classroom setting with impressionable and capable students. The book is extensively researched concerning the highs and lows of current teaching and learning approaches used in many schools and trusts. Above all, the intention is unclouded – it is essential for educators to understand their impact outside of a rigid and standardised curriculum. The book is not only accessible but broad. Each chapter provides a very original perspective on current secondary education practices within English education, and many instances have been discussed as to why critical pedagogy should be absorbed and practised in secondary education. Coles' experience working with students from marginalised and disadvantaged areas of society shines through the essence of this book. As a former student, I positively attest to the philosophy and promotion of self-emancipation this book encapsulates. At a time when politics is a back-seat but powerful driver of education, this book is not only timely but influential.

K. Devi, former student

Tait Coles is an intellectual. Some time ago, he was the great 'white' hope of the left of the profession, and I am delighted he's returned to publish his critical perspective on critical pedagogy. Coles is enormously well read and, consequently, his thoughts on the subject are deeply well-articulated, fluid and immensely politically astute. At a time when pedagogic culture is dominated by chancers and lightweights, it is a joy to read something from an important voice that has come to the fore once again. I look forward to reading more of his leftist wisdoms and learnings in the mid- and long-term future.

Phil Beadle, teacher, author and speaker

ACKNOWLEDGEMENTS

I would like to dedicate this book to my beautiful wife, Rachel, and our two amazing children, Hugh and Lydia. Without their love I would not be the person I am today.

I would like to thank everyone who took time to review this book, in particular Sadia Habib and Henry Giroux, who have constantly supported and encouraged me over the years. Thank you both. A big appreciation must also be given to my editor, Isla McMillan.

Throughout the process of writing this book I have been inspired by the words and music of the following artists: Damon Albarn, David Byrne, Matt Johnson, Phil Judd, Kevin Rowland, Mark E. Smith and Joe Strummer.

Finally, this book is for the hundreds of students I have had – and continue to have – the privilege of teaching and learning from.

CONTENTS

PREFACE

In Robert Tressell's seminal novel *The Ragged Trousered Philanthropists*, first published in 1914, a conversation develops between a group of workers. The men are carpenters, plumbers, plasterers, bricklayers, painters and unskilled labourers. During their lunch break, one of the characters, reading a newspaper report on unemployment, poverty and the government's strategies to tackle these issues, opens up the conversation.

> 'Wot do you think of this 'ere fissical policy, Bob?'

> 'Ain't thought much about it,' replied Crass. 'I don't never worry my 'ed about politics.'

The men discuss the state of their fictional town of Mugsborough, the state of their country and the causes of poverty. They debate reasons including alcohol, early marriage, overpopulation, 'foreigners' (Tressell, 2004), new machinery that puts skilled people out of work and, finally, education.

> 'In my opinion ther's too much of this 'ere eddication, nowadays,' remarked old Linden. 'Wot the 'ell's the good of eddication to the likes of us?'

WHAT THE HELL IS THE GOOD OF EDUCATION TO THE LIKES OF US?

The educationalist Dylan Wiliam has suggested that one of the purposes of education is 'cultural transmission' (Wiliam, 2017). Many educators agree with this, believing that the aim of education is to increase students' knowledge acquisition and build their cultural literacy. E.D. Hirsch, Jr, the founder and chair of the Core Knowledge Foundation, promotes this idea of cultural literacy in the form of his Core Knowledge Sequence curriculum guidelines for the US. Hirsch advocates for a curriculum based on a common body of knowledge. In his 1987 book *Cultural Literacy*, he identified 5,000 elements of knowledge that every American student should know.

In a 2015 essay for the right-wing think tank Policy Exchange, Nick Gibb, then UK schools minister, explained how 'Hirsch's work in America provided us with a tangible precedent for our thinking on the English National Curriculum' (Gibb, 2015a). This approach is now being replicated in many English secondary schools. Natasha Porter and Jonathan Simons, then the heads of education at Policy Exchange, wrote that Hirsch's ideas had significantly influenced Gibb and the former education secretary Michael Gove, and that 'Hirsch has had a profound impact on educational policy reform in England since the 2010 election' (Porter & Simons, 2015).

Hirsch suggests that cultural literacy benefits students as it 'enables them to take up a newspaper and read it with an adequate level of comprehension' (Hirsch, 1987).

While reading a fictional Tory newspaper, *The Obscurer*, one of Tressell's characters, Easton, declares:

> *'Well, I don't go in for politics much, either, but if what's in this 'ere paper is true, it seems to me as we oughter take some interest in it, when the country is being ruined by foreigners.'*

Traditional and authoritative methods of education, where teachers impart selected knowledge to students, not only ignore young people's existing knowledge and experiences but also prevent any possibility of emancipation (liberation from restrictions, control and power). By contrast, critical pedagogy can harness the tools necessary to liberate marginalised communities, by catalysing students to critique the social world, become politically astute, and transform their own lives and society. Critical pedagogy is participatory, empowering and interactive. It demands that classrooms should aspire to be sites of struggle, with opportunities for resistance and critique, thus capturing moments of hope and possibility, and forming the beginnings of social change.

If we want young people to be aware of their world, we must teach them about their world. Students' thoughts, opinions and values are predominantly influenced by two main sources: media and education, including information gained from families, friends and schools. Social and traditional media (TV and newspapers) can undoubtedly shape minds. As teachers, we have little or no control over the media that is absorbed by our students. However, we do have influence over the education they receive in schools. We may not have the ascendancy to determine *what* we teach, but we do have a legitimate agency about *how* we teach.

The purpose of education will always be the subject of ongoing and nuanced debate, yet the importance of education should never be doubted. However, there will always be individuals who suggest that education is not important. Back to *The Ragged Trousered Philanthropists*, where Crass replies to Linden's question:

'Wot the 'ell's the good of eddication to the likes of us?'

'None whatever,' said Crass, 'it just puts foolish idears into people's 'eds and makes 'em too lazy to work.'

INTRODUCTION

Critical Pedagogy: a teacher's companion has been written to promote and inspire dialogue and thinking. It will always be an ambitious and difficult challenge to fundamentally alter the way someone teaches, or encourage them to change their assumptions and opinions about education. This book aims to influence new thinking and invite debate, even if it's initially the internal dialogue of the reader. Throughout the pages there are important questions for the teacher and school leader to consider. These questions can also be used as starting points for discussions among committed educators.

Critical pedagogy inspires teachers to develop an authentic and formative dialogical classroom culture for all their students. A culture that embodies a moral, ethical and political endeavour. Critical pedagogy emphasises teaching and learning that catalyse a desire from students (particularly those from marginalised areas of society) to become critically aware, politically knowledgeable and socially responsible. This critical reflection and consciousness will promote a form of self-emancipation for our students, with the ultimate goal of creating a fairer and more equitable society for themselves and others.

This introduction will focus on two important questions. First, what is critical pedagogy? I will dispel some of the myths and misconceptions about critical pedagogy and discuss criticisms of this approach to teaching and learning. I will also suggest that critical pedagogy should be advocated not just in further and higher education but also in secondary schooling. The second question is: why is there a need for critical pedagogy? I will invite the reader to consider the urgency of critical pedagogy (alluded to in the preface) and highlight its key thinkers and advocates, encouraging further investigation through recommended reading.

WHAT IS CRITICAL PEDAGOGY?

Critical pedagogy is a transformational approach to education that moves beyond the transmission model of teaching. Paulo Freire, whom we will discuss later in the introduction, described this as a 'banking' model of teaching (Freire, 1996) and equated teachers with bank clerks. In this model, teachers deposit selected amounts of prescribed information into students, rather than harnessing meaning and understanding from individuals, or developing inquisitive beings with a hunger for knowledge. Freire describes this as a 'characteristic of the ideology of oppression', where the knowledge is seen as a gift *from* the knowledgeable teacher *to* the ignorant student. He writes that many teachers seem to be 'unshakably convinced that it is their mission to "give" [students] their knowledge and techniques ... Their programs of action ... include their own objectives, their own convictions, and their own preoccupations' (Freire, 1996). According to Freire, the banking model not only 'negates education and knowledge as processes of inquiry', but when the teacher believes that students are ill-informed and ignorant 'he justifies his own existence'.

At this point I would like to address Freire's use of patriarchal terms. The author and educator bell hooks writes: 'There has never been a moment when reading Freire that I have not remained aware of ... the sexism of the language' (hooks, 1993). Although a simplistic argument can be made about the time when Freire wrote his book, 'from a feminist perspective, *Pedagogy of the Oppressed* is striking in its male referent' (Weiler, 1994). hooks writes: 'For me this is always a source of anguish for it represents a blind spot in the vision of men who have profound insight' (hooks, 1993). When we advocate for the benefits of and need for critical pedagogy, we must be conscious of all the marginalised groups that it seeks to liberate, including our female students.

In his book *The Schools We Need and Why We Don't Have Them*, E.D. Hirsch, Jr claims that an 'intellectual capacity' is necessary for 'the oppressed classes to learn how to read, write, and communicate – and to gain enough traditional knowledge to understand the worlds of nature and culture surrounding them' (Hirsch, 1996). On initial reading, it seems that Hirsch's view of education is supportive and respectful of the 'oppressed classes'. However, we need to interrogate the words 'enough' and 'traditional'. How do we quantify what is *enough* knowledge? What is deemed as traditional knowledge? Is this traditional knowledge valued more highly than other forms of knowledge? And, importantly, who defines this traditional knowledge?

As the educational theorist Michael Apple argues, 'the decision to define some groups' knowledge as the most legitimate, as official knowledge, while other groups' knowledge hardly sees the light of day, says something extremely important about who has power in society' (Apple, 1993). We should be clear on the distinction between learning knowledge to develop a genuine understanding and simply gathering and memorising information. The philosopher Antonio Gramsci believed that education should begin not from the point of view of the teacher but from that of the learner: 'The relationship between teacher and pupil is active and reciprocal so that every teacher is always a pupil and every pupil a teacher' (Gramsci, 1971). The learning process must be a movement towards self-knowledge, self-mastery and eventual self-liberation. Education is not a matter of handing out 'encyclopedic knowledge' (Gramsci, 1971) but of developing an authentic awareness, critical consciousness and determined agency in all our students.

Critical pedagogy enables the classroom to become an environment where the 'education of citizens might have some direct bearing on the well-being of the social and ecological places people actually inhabit' (Gruenewald, 2003). We need teachers who believe that every classroom should be a place of educational 'freedom and free initiative, not a school of slavery and mechanical precision'; a place where students 'should be able to develop their own individuality in the optimal way, and hence in the most productive way for both themselves and society' (Gramsci, 2000). The need for standardised information accumulation, and the apparent disregard of the cultures and histories of our students, forces marginalised and oppressed groups to learn about only the dominant culture. This is a deliberate strategy to reproduce and maintain the social order, often referred to as the hegemony of society, where certain groups are ascendant or dominant over others, typically through cultural, economic or political means. Allowing only specific knowledge that represents the dominant groups (usually white, middle class and male) to be learned in our schools fails to consider the values and beliefs of all our students.

Hirsch writes that 'the children of the poor, should not be encouraged to flourish naturally, which would keep them ignorant and make them slaves of emotion' (Hirsch, 1996). It appears that our students do not need and indeed should not be allowed to become emotionally connected with their learning. But learning should always start with an impulse. The execution of this impulse will lead to a desire. The end point of this impulse and desire is itself the purpose. To act on this impulse and achieve the purpose requires a vested interest in the knowledge being learned. Promoting a defined and stagnant 'intellectual capacity' (Hirsch, 1996) in classrooms separates facts from values and emotion from intellect. According to the writer and cultural critic Henry A. Giroux, Hirsch implies that 'teaching working class children about the specificities of their histories, experiences, and cultural memories would simply result in a form of pedagogical infantilism' (Giroux, 2011). Giroux goes on to say that 'Hirsch wants to "save" underprivileged kids by stripping them of their identities and histories'.

Learning that is centred around the experiences, contexts, cultures and histories of the students in a specific school will empower them to become critical and engaged agents, capable of making a change. However, the 'banking' education system much applauded and promoted in English secondary schools only 'serves the interests of the oppressors' (Freire, 1996) and conceals from learners a genuine and authentic view of the world. Thereby, an 'if it ain't broke, don't fix it' culture is preserved. There is a deliberate attempt to portray to our young people that they live in a society that is ultimately fair and equal and based on meritocracy.

Schools are increasingly becoming nondescript, standardised and uniform institutes – more like 'boot camps for the intellectually malleable' (Giroux, 2011) that douse any opportunities for creativity and uniqueness and produce isolated and politically ambiguous subordinates. How many of our schools are stimulating and educating their students to achieve a critical awareness of what is actually happening in their own world? Are schools energising young people to do something differently in their lifetime? How many of our teachers ignore the desires and impulses of their students in favour of simply 'bestowing the gift' (Freire, 1996) of their knowledge? For many students, 'the only escape from [traditional, authoritative and potentially stifling teaching methods] in a standardized school is an activity which is irregular and perhaps disobedient' (Dewey, 1938). Critical pedagogy is an ongoing moral project that enables young people to be challenged with the structured provocation of 'reorientation, redefinition and revisioning' of knowledge (Litner, 1990). This motivates students to not only think differently but also act differently. Students must be allowed to develop the qualities of civic courage, political literacy and social responsibility, and to learn to match these attributes with compassion, determination and articulation.

The pedagogy promoted by many secondary schools in the UK is a simple transmission model of teaching that instils a culture of conformity and passive absorption of regulated knowledge. It creates subordinate students devoid of critical thought, authentic questioning or a desire to challenge the assumptions, practices and ideas of the dominant culture. Only through a critical formative culture can students learn to become knowledgeable individuals and social agents, rather than merely disengaged spectators who have their part to play in an unequal and unfair society. In an email exchange between myself and Giroux, he wrote that the 'notion that knowledge should be meaningful in order to be critical and transformative is lost on those reformers who are really simply accountants of a neoliberal audit culture'. According to Freire, classrooms need to 'establish an "intimate" connection between knowledge considered basic to any school curriculum and knowledge that is the fruit of the lived experience of these students as individuals' (Freire, 1998). Only through this connected knowledge can students learn 'a course of intellectual self-defense to protect themselves from manipulation and control' (Chomsky, 1989).

Our students need an authentic understanding and the skills to act on that knowledge, in a form of emancipatory learning that allows them to connect with the problems and conflicts of their lives.

Teachers must help their students to become courageous and 'willing to struggle for a more just and democratic world' (Giroux, 2019), stimulating and educating their students to achieve a critical awareness. Teachers must be prepared to embrace a critical pedagogy that compassionately provokes students 'to take risks, to struggle with ongoing relations of power, to critically appropriate forms of knowledge that exist outside their immediate experience' (Simon, 1987) and to react and act in their moment in time.

WHY IS THERE A NEED FOR CRITICAL PEDAGOGY?

Many politicians and educational theorists believe that schools are dysfunctional and failing. I would argue that schools are intentionally designed to fail; to fail the marginalised students that critical pedagogy seeks to support. However, the critiques from these experts are not centred around how the education system oppresses students from subaltern[1] groups, but around how students are taught. In 2021, the former schools minister Nick Gibb wrote, as he exited the Department for Education in a cabinet reshuffle, 'For the first time, a Conservative Government systematically challenged the so-called "progressive" approach – an ideology which downgraded the importance of knowledge and academic rigour and which argued that children learn better through projects and through self-discovery ... than by teacher-led teaching' (Gibb, 2021). Gibb echoed the thoughts of Hirsch, who believes that schools are failing young people by adopting forms of progressive education such as 'project orientated, hands on, critical thinking and so-called democratic education, rather than a core curriculum of facts and information' (Hirsch, 1996).

A common criticism and misconception of critical pedagogy is that it 'involves teachers working with the knowledge pupils already have and with the knowledge pupils are able to discover independently' (Christodoulou, 2014). Anyone who argues that it is a 'Freirean discovery-based critical pedagogy' (ibid, 2014) where students aren't required or expected to learn new information simply does not understand the

---

1   In postcolonial theory, the term 'subaltern' describes the lower social classes and other social groups displaced to the margins of a society.

aims, methods and impact of critical pedagogy. To dismiss it as a form of emancipatory education is a considered approach from those 'who care neither to have the world revealed nor to see it transformed' (Freire, 1996). If society is changed, this would undoubtedly result in a power shift away from the established hierarchy. According to the UK government's 'behaviour tsar', Tom Bennett, who leads the Department for Education's behaviour hubs project, 'Criticism [sic] pedagogy is an ideology based on Marxism. I'm ok with teaching children about Marxism. I'm ok with them becoming Marxists. I'm not ok with teaching them to be Marxists' (Bennett, 2018). Many educationalists find little incentive in supporting a pedagogy that works to highlight and eradicate inequality, as they could ultimately find that their positions of perceived superiority, dominance and ascendancy are challenged.

Knowledge and information are essential to critical pedagogy. Freire, as detailed later in this introduction, devoted a significant part of his life to improving literacy among his fellow Brazilians. He argued that in order to understand the world, one must gain knowledge through reading: 'The actual act of reading literary texts is seen as part of a wider process of human development and growth' (Freire, 1983). And after learning to read the word, the next step is to use it to read the world. Knowledge and the learning of knowledge are prerequisites for critical pedagogy. We must afford all our students, regardless of their class, ethnicity or gender, the 'opportunity to read, write and learn from a position of agency – to engage in a culture of questioning that demands far more than competency in rote learning and the application of acquired skills' (Giroux, 2010). Critical pedagogy is not a form of discovery learning or independent learning, but rather a form of teaching and learning where teachers and students learn collaboratively and with a moral purpose. All our students need an education that prepares them with knowledge and the skills to act on that knowledge, allowing them to connect with the problems and conflicts of their lifetime and to develop the courage and responsibility to make a positive change.

Teachers have to recognise their duty in harnessing purposeful learning for social transformation. They must recognise that learning is a complex and nuanced process that goes far beyond simple drill-orientated and stimulus-and-response methodologies. We must move away from education that places a 'premium upon preserving the outward appearance of attention, decorum, and obedience', as this 'artificial uniformity' will ultimately 'prevent pupils from disclosing their real natures' (Dewey, 1938). Teachers should never ignore matters of context. The elements of culture, histories and meaning that all students own and bring to their school must be heard, valued and harnessed. Without stimulating a freedom from within our students, it is impossible for teachers to gain knowledge of the individuals they teach. The philosopher Simone de Beauvoir believed that a uniform traditional education is deliberate in 'changing the consciousness of the oppressed, not the situation which oppresses them' (De Beauvoir, 1955). She argued that the more the marginalised consumers of education are encouraged to accept and adapt to the situation they are in, the more easily they can be controlled. Critical pedagogy is always a political and moral act, one that allows all our students – including and especially our marginalised students – to learn from their world and about their world (and the real-life situation they are in) in order to gain the knowledge, attributes and agency to make the world a permanently fairer place for themselves and others.

Let's now look at the key thinkers and advocates of critical pedagogy. First, Paulo Freire, who is regarded as the founder of critical pedagogy.

PAULO FREIRE

Paulo Reglus Neves Freire was born in the city of Recife in north-eastern Brazil in 1921. Brazil, a Portuguese colony from 1500-1822, was primarily seen as a commercial economic venture that allowed the Portuguese (and the Dutch) to exploit its resources, mainly sugar but also gold and diamonds. 'Newspapers were not published in Brazil until 1808, and literacy among the vast majority of Brazilians was simply nonexistent' (Díaz, n.d). After its independence from Portugal in 1822, Brazil experienced a period of economic growth and the slavery of its indigenous people was finally abolished in 1888. However, even during Freire's early life, the social, economic and living conditions of many Brazilians were desperate. As Freire lived among the poor rural families and labourers of Recife, he gained a deep and authentic understanding of their lives and of the effects of the socioeconomics in Brazil. 'It was through these hardships that Freire developed his unyielding sense of solidarity with the poor. From childhood on, Freire made a conscious commitment to work in order to improve the conditions of marginalized people' (Díaz, n.d).

In an attempt to improve literacy among the people of his country, Freire began to teach Portuguese and adult literacy classes. In 1946, he was appointed director of education at Serviço Social da Indústria, an institution that still exists today and works 'to improve quality of education and to elevate the level of schooling of Brazilians'.[2] During this time, he started to see even more the 'disconnections between elitist educational practices and the real lives of the working class' (Bentley, 1999). In 1959, he wrote his PhD thesis, entitled *Present-day Education in Brazil*. Ultimately, 'his convictions would earn him the title of "traitor"' (Bentley, 1999). From 1962, Freire set up literacy projects, the first of which taught 300 farmworkers to read and write in 45 days. As a result, the Brazilian government approved thousands of educational centres to be established all over Brazil.

However, in 1964, a military coup supported by the CIA deposed Brazil's president, João Goulart. Goulart had been a populist leader at a time when a 'communist presence was more clearly felt in Brazil' and after his election 'many student groups, unions, and peasant leagues began to emerge' (Díaz, n.d). During the coup, Freire was removed from his position in the Cultural Extension Service at the University of Recife. The new military regime deemed Freire's literacy projects subversive, his teaching materials were confiscated and he was 'subjected to a series of interrogations and accused of being a communist' (Díaz, n.d). Freire spent more than 70 days in jail, where he began to write his first book, *Education as the Practice of Freedom*. After its publication in 1967, he was invited to be a visiting professor at Harvard University in the US.

The military coup forced Freire and his family into exile from Brazil until 1980. During this time, he lived in Bolivia and Chile, where he continued his literacy projects with Chilean farmers. While working as a teacher, Freire developed his lifelong goal to 'create the circumstances for his students to discover themselves as human beings, with their own

---

2   www.portaldaindustria.com.br/sesi/en/about/sesi

agency as subjects and not objects, as members of a community, and as the creators of culture' (Díaz, n.d). On his return to Brazil, he continued his work as an educator, taking on the roles of professor at the University of São Paulo, professor emeritus at the Federal University of Pernambuco, and secretary of education for the city of São Paulo in 1989. Freire left an unwavering legacy after his death in 1997, and his life and achievements continue to inspire. He 'created the conditions by which thousands of people, the children and grandchildren of former slaves, could learn to read and write, learn about their agency and freedom, and learn to love' (Díaz, n.d).

Freire's seminal book, *Pedagogy of the Oppressed*, is generally considered as the foundation text for what we now call critical pedagogy. This, his second book, was first published in Spanish in 1968 and in English in 1970. But owing to the political climate in Brazil, the book was only published in Brazil in 1974 and in the Portuguese language a year later. *Pedagogy of the Oppressed* was and still is influential all over the world and has been translated into 17 languages. In South Africa, it was 'banned by the white government because it was an important influence on black anti-apartheid activists' (Gannon, 2017). In 2012, the Tucson Unified School District in Arizona, US, 'banned Freire's *Pedagogy of the Oppressed* from its schools as part of a state-wide proscription of ethnic studies' (Wanberg, 2013). This was part of a 2010 state law that attempted to rein in 'pedagogical practices designed to raise social consciousness' (Wanberg, 2013). *Pedagogy of the Oppressed* continues to be a powerful, radical and revolutionary text that redefines the very idea and purpose of education.

Numerous scholars, educators, activists and writers have been influenced by Freire's life, achievements and ideas. Among these are Peter McLaren, Antonia Darder, Angela Valenzuela, Joe Kincheloe, Ira Shor, Michael Apple, Roger I. Simon and bell hooks.

BELL HOOKS

bell hooks was a teacher, author and contemporary feminist theorist who wrote extensively about issues of race, gender, class and education. She was born Gloria Jean Watkins in 1952, in Kentucky, US. Growing up in the segregated South, along with receiving 'almost no support from her family, who felt that women were better suited for a more traditional role' (Jankowski, 2021), initially discouraged her from pursuing her love of speaking and writing.

As a writer, she chose to use the pseudonym bell hooks, partly in tribute to her mother and great-grandmother, and decided 'not to capitalize her new name to place focus on her work rather than her name, on her ideas rather than her personality' (Quintana, 2010). By creating this other self, 'hooks empowered herself to fight back against the opposition that surrounded her' (Jankowski, 2021).

hooks lectured and wrote passionately on the need for intersectionality (recognition of the interconnected nature of race, class and gender) in education, and for education to be a practice of freedom. She saw the classroom as a 'location of possibility', but 'only if it was a dialogical space, in which both the student and the teacher were empowered' (Moreira da Silva, 2022). hooks published more than 40 books in her lifetime, most notably *Teaching to Transgress: education as the practice of freedom* (1994) and *Teaching Community: a pedagogy of hope* (2003). After a long illness, she died in 2021 at the age of 69. Her legacy and influence will be everlasting.

HENRY A. GIROUX

Professor Henry A. Giroux is one of today's leading scholars of critical pedagogy. Born in 1943 in Rhode Island, US, he studied history and began his career as a high school social sciences teacher. He is currently the Paulo Freire Distinguished Scholar in Critical Pedagogy at McMaster University in Canada. Giroux has been 'credited with pioneering the field of critical pedagogy, articulating throughout his archive a vision of education as a political, moral, and ethical practice', and his work has 'continually asked educators to reconsider how they teach, under what conditions they teach, and for what purpose'.[3]

Giroux encourages the teacher to see their role 'not as a deskilled intellectual, but as a risk-taking, critical agent who brings issues of equity, community, and social justice to the educational arena' (Culp, 2014). He is

---

3   mi.mcmaster.ca/whoweworkwith/instructors-faculty-and-staff/distinguished-scholars-program

greatly inspired by the ideas of Freire, whom he worked alongside for many years. Giroux is undoubtedly one of the most important contemporary activists and thinkers, and has himself inspired many scholars, writers and teachers (myself included) to look to critical pedagogy to strengthen the 'construction of democratic values in public life' (Figueiredo et al., 2021). He is a prolific writer and has authored more than 70 books, including *Theory and Resistance in Education: towards a pedagogy for the opposition* (1983), *Teachers as Intellectuals: toward a critical pedagogy of learning* (1988), *On Critical Pedagogy* (2011) and *Pedagogy of Resistance: against manufactured ignorance* (2022). His most recent book is *Insurrections: education in an age of counter-revolutionary politics* (2023).

ABOUT THIS BOOK

Although it is recommended that *Critical Pedagogy: a teacher's companion* is read from cover to cover in order, each of the four chapters has been written as a separate entity, to encourage thinking about key themes pertinent to critical pedagogy.

Chapter 1 considers neutrality. It explores how teachers are becoming depoliticised in their profession, and embraces the idea that teachers must remain political in their pursuit of authentic critical pedagogy to inspire younger generations to change society for the better. This chapter argues that education should never be non-partisan, and that teachers must explore what it means to be neutral, both politically and morally.

Chapter 2 looks at teaching. It considers the current transmission model of teaching through basic, didactic and authoritative behavioural drills in the classroom. This chapter discusses the role of the teacher as a transformative intellectual who should deploy a professional resistance to move away from being a deskilled technician of content who simply transmits selected knowledge.

Chapter 3 explores narratives, investigating how critical pedagogy provides authentic opportunities for students to interrogate how mainstream and dominant narratives operate, and how counter-narratives can work as the antithesis to this false democracy. This chapter allows the reader to begin to understand the importance of critical race theory, a key principle of which is allowing hidden voices to be heard, listened to and valued.

Chapter 4 considers emancipation, exploring the importance of collective responsibility and agency, and delving into the difference between emancipation and self-emancipation. It concludes by focusing on how teachers must embrace risk and have the personal attributes of hope and possibility in order for critical pedagogy to be as sustainable and effective as it can be.

Each chapter provides the reader with an original perspective on current secondary education in English schools. The book openly discusses and professionally critiques approaches in teaching and learning that have been and are being used in many schools and trusts. It explores how critical pedagogy can be adopted as a different approach that encourages young people to develop a critical consciousness of the world they live in, and to relentlessly question and challenge the ideas of perceived meritocracy and fairness in society. This critical understanding will enable students to see how power operates in their world and its impacts on social equalities and social justice. Only then can our students use this knowledge and awareness to challenge these inequalities and injustices.

This book is not a guidebook, nor a manual, but a teacher's companion. A common critique of critical pedagogy is that it often lacks concrete examples and practices that can be implemented by a classroom teacher. Although it must be acknowledged that critical pedagogy is not a prescribed method that can be simply applied to any situation regardless of context, *Critical Pedagogy: a teacher's companion* will provide realistic and pragmatic suggestions that I have tried and tested in secondary schools. Thus, the reader will have opportunities to reflect on the key concepts of the book and decide on ways to move from the theory of critical pedagogy into actual practice – or praxis – in their own classroom. This will empower the classroom teacher (and school leader) to successfully implement critical pedagogy as a continued and responsive endeavour.

WHY HAVE I WRITTEN THIS BOOK

I have been a teacher of science and a school leader for 20 years. Throughout my educational career, I have chosen to work predominantly in Bradford, where I also happily live. I have worked in secondary schools that have allowed me to experience various forms of school culture, behaviour management principles, and teaching and learning strategies. I have worked in schools in 'outstanding' multi-academy trusts, as well as schools that Ofsted classed as 'good', 'requires improvement' and 'special measures' (now referred to as 'inadequate'). During this time, I have had the privilege to learn with, and from, thousands of young people. Many of these students would be classed as coming from a social or economic disadvantage. Most of the schools that I have chosen to work in predominantly serve Muslim students, mainly of working-class South Asian heritage. However, I have also worked with and continue to work alongside students from White British, Eastern European and Black African backgrounds. I therefore have considerable experience of witnessing and challenging inequalities in education and society. My writing is not a criticism of the schools I have worked in or currently work in. Rather, this book critiques secondary education and schools in England in general.

While writing and researching my first book, *Never Mind the Inspectors: here's punk learning* (2014), I read more and more about critical pedagogy. The writings of Freire, Giroux, hooks, Simon and others provoked me to look at teaching and education in a different way. I was able to dissect my role as a teacher and as a learner. I interrogated my assumptions, values and principles. I continue to do this every day when I stand in front of – and with – all my students. I no longer see my role primarily as a knowledgeable informer and conductor of content for my students.

I am proud to write that, throughout my career, I have supported and educated my students to achieve academic success. I have a proven track record of impact on student attainment and progress for the students that I teach and have taught. I work relentlessly to ensure that every student in my classroom achieves or exceeds their academic potential. However, critical pedagogy has allowed me to consider that education is much more than this. Through my research, reading and practice, critical pedagogy has catalysed a moral and political purpose in me to highlight the issues of societal inequality and injustice compassionately and sensitively.

I have seen first-hand the effect that critical pedagogy has had on my students. I have collaboratively worked with cohorts of students to enable them to develop a sustained social awareness and a critical consciousness.

When I have given my students opportunities to safely and openly articulate their opinions and feelings, I have experienced the eradication of the traditional hierarchical structures between teacher and students. I have observed the emancipatory nature of encouraging Muslim students to speak to a (white, non-Muslim) teacher about their own lives. I have witnessed my students appreciate the power of their own narratives in challenging inequalities and inspiring social change. I have been proud to hear about ex-students who are involved in campaigns and activism, such as Speakers Corner in Bradford, a collective of women and girls who bring people together to create positive action. I have met and been contacted by individuals whom I had the privilege to teach, who have told me about their successes and continued desire to make social and community change happen.

However, I am an onlooker of the transformative impact of critical pedagogy. I am an outsider, seeing how students are affected by inequality and disparity in society. I personally do not suffer from the institutionalised discrimination that I witness in everyday life. And here lies the issue that needs some discussion. I benefit, and have always benefited, from my white, male, straight, middle-class and able-bodied privilege. For example, I have never suffered or had to fight against any form of racism or sexism. And it took me a long time to realise this. So, can I legitimately write about the emancipatory nature of critical pedagogy? David Gillborn, emeritus professor of critical race studies at Birmingham University, discusses the idea of 'egotistical posturing' (Gillborn, 2008), when commentary and criticism occur simply to fuel and promote a sense of self-satisfaction and delusions of grandeur. However, I believe there is a distinction between a committed educator raising important issues of inequality in society and a self-serving endeavour. As bell hooks writes, 'To engage in dialogue is one of the simplest ways we can begin as teachers, scholars, and critical thinkers to cross boundaries, the barriers that may or may not be erected by race, gender, class, professional standing, and a host of other differences … If we really want to create a cultural climate where biases can be challenged and changed, all border crossings must be seen as valid and legitimate' (hooks, 1994).

My reason for writing *Critical Pedagogy: a teacher's companion* is to support and help other teachers to recognise the existence of inequality and the marginalisation of certain young people (owing to their ethnicity, class, religion and background) in education and in society in general.

WHO IS THIS BOOK FOR?

This book is for the teacher new to the profession who embodies the moral purpose of educating young people. The book is also for the teacher disillusioned by the current state of secondary education in England. More and more teachers are leaving the profession. Many are feeling the pressure to be part of the transmission model of teaching that results in the passive absorption of knowledge, creating a culture of conformity for students but also teachers. Additionally, this book is for the busy teacher who has the inclination and ability but not the time to read heavy academic texts on critical pedagogy. One criticism of critical pedagogy is that it is often explained in an abstract way, sometimes in the form of dense academic prose. It is important to consider that this transformational method of teaching is a complex, nuanced and sophisticated process, which is why writing on critical pedagogy is often exactly that. However, what critical pedagogy is, what it stands for and its ultimate goals can be presented clearly and concisely. This book will reference key thinkers and oppositional viewpoints to enable the reader to further investigate critical pedagogy and to explore their own understanding. Finally, this book is for teachers who are advocates of critical pedagogy but have lost hope and focus.

CHAPTER 1
NEUTRALITY

The relationship between a student and teacher needs to be strong and authentic. It changes constantly and requires fluidity. Teachers should regularly ask important questions about this relationship. For example, what do my students think of me? Do my students know what I stand for? Would they be able to say what I believe in? As Paulo Freire suggests, educators 'cannot escape being evaluated by the students, and the way they evaluate me is of significance for my modus operandi as a teacher' (Freire, 1998). When a student evaluates their teacher, they begin to develop a form of mutual respect and trust within the relationship, as well as forging a collective purpose for their shared learning.

Critical pedagogues believe that a teacher's role is more than simply imparting academic knowledge. Writing about the purpose of education, bell hooks argues that students should learn not just designated curriculum knowledge 'but knowledge about how to live in the world' (hooks, 1994). Critical pedagogy enables young people to become conscious and active citizens. This is preferable to their remaining as 'disengaged spectators who have their "part to play" in the neoliberal ideology of modern schooling' (Coles, 2014a). However, critical pedagogy is only effective when an authentic, symbiotic relationship of respect and understanding exists between teacher and student in the classroom.

THE POLITICAL TEACHER

The teacher is a learner too. The teacher seeks to understand what their students believe in and what they stand for, thus stimulating students' agency and authority. However, teachers need the confidence and opportunities to communicate to their students who they are and what they believe in. After all, 'I cannot be a teacher without exposing who I am. Without revealing, either reluctantly or with simplicity, the way I relate to the world, how I think politically' (Freire, 1998). This chapter explores the idea that allowing your students to understand you is as important as your understanding them, and an essential part of this understanding is knowing how you think politically.

Neutrality, meaning the absence of decided views, expression or strong feelings, can come from political illiteracy, political apathy (the strongest of all emotions) or a naive political ignorance. Teachers who are learning about critical pedagogy must realise that education never is, nor should be, neutral. As Henry A. Giroux suggests, the 'defence of neutrality has always seemed to me to be the basis for a kind of fascist politics because it hides its code for not allowing people to understand the role that education plays ideologically' (França, 2019). Education has an essential power to transform the world into a fairer, more compassionate and more democratic place. As educators, we need to be aware that models of pedagogy can themselves suggest an act of neutrality. If the knowledge that is taught to young people is filtered and selected, only certain knowledge is learned. If knowledge is taught in a subjective and reductive way, only certain narratives are given weight and importance (often hegemonic ones – the dominant viewpoints in a political or social context). These ideas are discussed in more detail in chapter 2.

Teachers must explore what it means to be neutral, politically and indeed morally. For example, if a teacher displays neutral and apolitical views about significant world events, some students might perceive this neutrality as a lack of awareness or duty of care. Neutrality, or perceived neutrality, can have negative impacts, particularly on students' sense of belonging in your classroom.

Below is an excerpt from a blog post[4] I wrote after the horrific tragedy in Paris on Friday 13 November 2015. Gunmen and suicide bombers attacked a concert hall, a stadium, restaurants and bars, leaving 130

---

4   taitcoles.wordpress.com/2015/11/15/a-message-to-our-students-after-the-paris-tragedy

people dead and hundreds wounded. The blog post was written over the weekend, when the media coverage was unfolding, and it sums up my initial thoughts. The piece is very raw. Looking back at my writing nine years later, I stand by every word of it. It was intended to be read by educators, mainly non-Muslim teachers, to help them consider what they should say to their Muslim students after the event.

> *I'm writing this in the aftermath of the horrific and chilling events from Paris. Needless to say that all my thoughts are with the families and friends that have lost their loved ones during the devastating tragedy that occurred in the late hours of Friday night.*
>
> *Why am I writing this post? Well, this is for all the educators who will return to their schools and classes on Monday morning still with the sad possibility that the death toll may have increased. This is a post to encourage teachers and leaders to think about their approach and how they will discuss the Paris tragedy with their students.*
>
> *Firstly, let's think about how mainstream media – the media that our students may possibly consume – have reported the events and also the thoughts, opinions and feelings that are being freely expressed on social media. It is one thing that our students will be subjected to the uncensored racist dirge and ill-informed bigotry that riddles social media, but should students – without our help – assume that all the news coverage they see and hear is completely partisan and without political gain? For example, we will need to explain to our students that linking the Paris attacks with the rise of refugees in France is hideously inaccurate (Applebaum, 2015). We must also explain to our students, and be honest with ourselves, that Western foreign policy has had a detrimental effect and caused more deaths. Without the invasion of Iraq, there would be no Islamic State (Oborne, 2015), which has claimed responsibility for the horror in Paris. If the ultimate goals of these terrorist attacks are to create hostility, hatred and separation between Muslims and non-Muslims in France and other Western countries then we are already witnessing and seeing the Islamophobic backlash (Press Association, 2015). Our students must understand that after witnessing evil hate, we must combat it with compassion, solidarity and understanding.*

> Secondly, it needs to be highlighted that although the events in Paris were obviously acts of hideous violence, where was the outrage when 43 people lost their lives in Beirut on Thursday? Or, indeed, where was the vocal mourning for the 26 people who lost their lives in Baghdad? Where are the Lebanese flag Twitter ribbons? Where are the 'Solidarity for Beirut' hashtags? Where are the coloured lights on buildings indicating support and togetherness for the desolated families in Lebanon and Iraq?
>
> It is also essential for our students to realise that terrorist acts – similar to those seen in Paris, Beirut and Baghdad – kill tens and hundreds of people in places such as Palestine and Syria every single day. Let's be confident to discuss with our students: when does another dead body become more important than others? Is it only Western or white bodies that deserve our attention and our thoughts (Fares, 2015)? We should mourn for the lives lost in Paris, but perhaps we should also interrogate and think about why we don't mourn for lives lost elsewhere.
>
> Thirdly, under no circumstance should our Muslim students apologise or feel that they need to apologise for events such as the one in Paris. Spend less time in stating the bloody obvious that ISIS/Daesh do not represent Islam and more time reassuring our young Muslim pupils that they don't need to feel ashamed of their identity, religion and beliefs.

A few days after the blog post had been published, an anonymous comment appeared:

> I wish you were my teacher when 9/11 happened, or at least a face I knew and could turn to when I got abused at school. Over a decade later I am now seeing history repeat itself with a member of my family at ... the same school I attended all those years ago.

Teachers needed to talk to the young people in their care about the horrific events that took place in Paris in November 2015. However, many wouldn't. Many couldn't. And many thought that they shouldn't. The comment left on my blog post suggests that we always should.

TWO BENNS DON'T MAKE A RIGHT

In December 2015, soon after the Paris attacks, MPs voted in the House of Commons on whether the UK should join the US-led coalition air strikes against Islamic State militants in Syria. There was a 10-hour debate before the vote, in which MPs from all the UK's major political parties expressed their thoughts. Politicians who opposed the air strikes forecast untold damage and potentially worse consequences. Despite these dangers and concerns, MPs overwhelmingly backed the air strikes, by 397 votes to 223. A total of 66 Labour MPs sided with the Conservative government.

In 2017, it was reported by the UK-based Syrian Observatory for Human Rights that 'at least 33 people have been killed in an air strike on a school sheltering displaced people near the Isis-held city of Raqqa, Syria' (Osborne, 2017). The observatory believed that the US-led coalition, with support from the UK vote, had carried out the attack. This was just one example of the irreparable damage and tragic loss of life that resulted from the vote.

Many media outlets, on both the left and the right, decided to focus their reporting not so much on the outcome of the parliamentary vote in 2015 but rather on the passionate rhetoric of Hilary Benn, then the shadow foreign secretary. Colonel Tim Collins wrote in *The Telegraph* that the speech was 'one of the great orations in our Parliament and ... an inspiring example of a leader stepping forward in the face of adversity' (Collins, 2015). *How* Benn had expressed his thoughts, rather than what he actually said, became the focus. 'Not only was it passionate, it also came with a tempo and body language that made it spine-tingling ... above all it was inspiring,' wrote Collins. However, Benn spoke about deaths as collateral damage and as unfortunate yet necessary losses of life.

To illustrate the point, consider a speech made by Hilary Benn's late father, the socialist Labour MP Tony Benn, in 1998. He argued against bombing in Iraq and highlighted that politicians and 'military men are clever' as 'they talk not about people but about collateral damage' (Benn, 1998). He warned MPs of the innocent people who would be killed if they voted to bomb Iraq: 'Aren't Arabs terrified? Aren't Iraqis terrified?

Don't Arab and Iraqi women weep when their children die?' Tony Benn's speech suggested that all innocent people are just as precious as each other, regardless of where they live or where they come from.

Hilary Benn's speech, however, seemed to indicate that 'our' UK children were more valuable and more deserving of concern, care and love than children from other countries. This was illustrated by his comment that 'if it had happened here, they could have been our children' (Benn, 2015). His emotive rhetoric compared lives and deaths to encourage a moral decision on whether the UK should support the bombing of Syrian citizens. In this instance, grief seemed to have a geographical and racial hierarchy.

We live at a time when compassion is a dirty word in politics, humanitarian approaches seem like weak points of view, and so-called morality appears to ignore, or even support, the deaths of innocent people. Arguments become binary, with nuances and complexities deliberately ignored. And anyone who argues for further discussions on whether to bomb people in another country is accused of being a 'terrorist sympathiser' (Watt, 2015). If we look at the media coverage of terrorist attacks and the resulting government strategies, it seems that there is a political ranking of which bodies are more expendable. Elie Fares, a Lebanese physician and writer, suggests that 'there is a sense that we are not as important, that our lives are not as worthy' (Fares, 2015). It would appear, for example, that white European citizens are more important than brown people from the Middle East. Or that Muslims are not as important as people of other faiths. This is obviously a ridiculous notion for any moral educator who teaches young Muslims. But do your Muslim students know what you believe? This is an important question that educators must ask themselves on a regular basis.

If your Muslim students hear you discuss terrorist attacks, condemn the factually incorrect reporting of such atrocities and interrogate inhumane foreign policy, they will recognise that you are supporting them. With the aid of their teacher as a critical pedagogue, students can respond to the deepest problems and conflicts of their time. Teachers can ensure that their teaching is associated with the current social and political issues that their students are engaged with in their everyday lives. As hooks describes, a 'commitment to engaged pedagogy is an expression of political activism', one that requires the educator to make a 'choice to work against the grain, to challenge the status quo' (hooks, 1994). Of course, it is always difficult to challenge and ultimately dismantle deep-rooted inequalities. It will never be easy, as a teacher, to attempt to interrogate and change embedded structures of neutrality, and this work requires resilience and determination. As Roger I. Simon writes, teachers embarking on critical pedagogy 'have to be prepared for a sizable investment of time and energy in an activity that will likely require battles for legitimisation and be inherently conflictual' (Simon, 1992).

Working 'against the grain' (hooks, 1994) has become even more difficult since 2022, when the Department for Education published guidance explaining the legal requirements relating to political impartiality in schools. These instructions are a deliberate attempt to ensure that teachers display and embody a position of neutrality. However, the teacher deploying critical awareness and critical pedagogy approaches can work within these requirements. A DfE blog post discussing the guidance poses the question, 'Does this mean teachers aren't allowed to talk about politics in the classroom?' It responds, 'Teachers absolutely can talk about politics – and they are encouraged to do so' and also says that 'teaching about political issues and the differing views on these is an essential part of the curriculum' (Department for Education, 2022a). The blog post delivers the important message that 'some concepts and views are shared principles which underpin our society and should be reinforced by schools', including 'fundamental rights, tolerance and challenging discrimination and prejudice'. The political teacher, deploying critical pedagogy in their classroom, must agree that the dialogue and discussions encouraged in this chapter are exactly what is demanded by the guidance.

TRUTH UNCONTAMINATED BY POWER

As educators, we need to bridge the gap between what we say and what we do; 'between what I seem to be and what I am actually becoming' (Freire, 1998). Teachers who talk of a moral purpose in education must ensure that their pedagogical practices are in fact political and emancipatory. However, we must remember that it is a difficult choice to not be neutral and commit to discuss political views. Teachers must harness an eloquent resistance and a genuine desire to fight inequality and oppression. The law states that 'teachers must not promote partisan political views' (Department for Education, 2022a) but there has never been a more important time for educators to shun neutrality.

In 2015, I had the privilege of researching and writing an academic paper with a friend and colleague, Dr Nasima Hassan. The paper was called 'Misrepresentation: a qualitative study on discourses on Islam, British values and identity affecting British Muslim pupils in Bradford and East London' (Coles & Hassan, 2017). Part of the study looked at how Muslim students believed they were portrayed and represented in the media. Below are excerpts from some of the student responses that were given in interviews and discussions with me. Students were happy to give their names, ages and how they identified.

> 'I despise the media for what they do, as they make all Muslims seem as terrorists' – Adnaan, British-Pakistani, 15

> 'I feel like the media is painting all of the 1.6 billion Muslims with the same brush, which I find highly disrespectful. It's propaganda ... it's meant to be a trusted source, but it isn't. The media is a powerful weapon of mass destruction!' – Zak, Libyan, 16

> 'I get angry and frustrated that I get associated with the evil that is shown in the media about Muslims. I feel like there is a false portrayal of the religion due to the media and the way it targets Islam, therefore people aren't learning about it but they're being brainwashed into a biased view on Islam as a whole. It's definitely getting worse. It's almost like a habit for the media to portray Muslims as they do' – Akenyia, British-Muslim, 16

These excerpts capture the students' frustration and anger about media misrepresentation of Muslims and Islam. The comments also show how they had begun to analyse and deconstruct the media's power. My students spoke passionately about media misinterpretation and how it affected their lives socially and personally.

For me, the research study and discussions with my students illustrated the power of dialogue. After the informal interviews, one student asked me, 'Sir, when can we do this again?' – an example of the traditional hierarchical structure between teacher and student being 'completely eradicated from the process due to the very nature of the opportunity given to students to openly articulate their opinions and thoughts' (Coles & Hassan, 2017). Although authority was still present during these conversations, my students were given the opportunity to speak to a (white, non-Muslim) teacher about their own lives. This was 'an emancipatory act, as the tables were turned and a shift of power took place very early on in the interviews' (Coles & Hassan, 2017). The students were afforded the privilege by their teacher of discussing truth uncontaminated by power. By creating opportunities for dialogue, 'demystifying' (Biesta, 2013) was allowed to happen. Demystifying, through discussion, helps students to reveal what is hidden – overtly and covertly – from the everyday views of those being oppressed. 'We cannot assume that this kind of knowledge and understanding will "come" to them simply by being exposed to the "realities" of the work world' (Simon, 1992). Only when teachers demystify the truth and encourage the ownership of knowledge by our students will their paths become clear. As the writer and civil rights activist James Baldwin wrote, 'The precise role of the artist is to illuminate that darkness, blaze roads through that vast forest, so that we will not, in all our doing, lose sight of its purpose, which is, after all, to make the world a more human dwelling place' (Baldwin, 1962).

IDENTITY, LABELS AND OTHERING

Through critical pedagogy, teachers can value their students' experiences, activate their critical consciousness and integrate their backgrounds into genuine and transformative learning experiences in the classroom. However, to do this, teachers must ensure that young people are aware of power structures outside the classroom that may limit and devalue their experiences and identities. In his book *Multiculturalism*, Tariq Modood suggests that it's possible – and necessary – for students to turn a negative label into a positive identity. He refers to this as an 'assertive identity statement' where 'an oppressed group challenges not just its oppression but the prevailing wisdom about its mode of oppression' (Modood, 2013).

This type of thinking is core to critical race theory, which will be discussed in chapter 3. The teacher can support this 'self-realisation' among their students (Simon, 1992) and their interrogation of power and authority, thus catalysing agency and freedom. This itself is an emancipatory act, which will be explored further in chapter 4.

It is often difficult to understand, or begin to understand, a student's identity. Some young people are very confident about how their sense of self-identity interacts with social factors such as friendships, faith and schooling. Other students may feel hesitation in visibly displaying their identity, but this is a natural pathway of identity exploration – 'a search that is an essential part of growing up, but could also stem from a fear of being labelled as an "other"' (Coles & Hassan, 2017). At this juncture, it is useful to consider what we mean by identity. It is also important to recognise how the meaning of 'identity' has changed over time. Stuart Hall argues that the identities that once stabilised the social world are now in decline, 'giving rise to new identities' (Hall, 1996). We must always consider that individual identities are 'never unified', but are 'increasingly fragmented and fractured; never singular but multiply constructed across different, often intersecting and antagonistic, discourses, practices and positions' (Hall, 1996). Educators must always analyse student identities in conjunction with histories, languages and cultures. It is essential that we recognise that our students' identities are constantly in flux – a transformational process of becoming 'not "who we are" or "where we came from", so much as what we might become, how we have been represented and how that bears on how we might represent ourselves' (Hall, 1996).

If identity can be described as the unique identifying characteristics that allow us to be represented and recognised, we must also interrogate how others may see us. A label can be described as a classifying term, applied either to individuals or to a group of people, that is often inaccurate or restrictive. If, as an example, we look at how Muslim students are often labelled, teachers can interrogate homogeneous collective labels that are imposed upon groups of young Muslims through 'preconceived ideas and at times typecasting' (Ahmed, 2009). Such labelling will result in negativity toward groups of Muslims, a reluctance to celebrate the individual identities of Muslims and, worryingly, an increase in racism and Islamophobia.

Government strategies to combat terrorism have normalised the collective prerogative labelling of Muslims. According to Open Society Foundations, the Prevent strategy has created 'a risk of discrimination, particularly against Muslims. Frontline professionals have broad discretion to act on their conscious or unconscious biases in deciding whom to report under Prevent'. Implicit biases can be galvanised by labelling. A climate of Islamophobia in which Muslims are labelled as potential extremists or even terrorists 'creates the risk that Muslims in particular may be erroneously targeted under Prevent' (Open Society Foundations, 2016). As well as reinforcing dangerous labelling, the Prevent duty has 'created a significant chilling effect on freedom of expression in schools and universities, and undermined trust between teachers and students' (Open Society Foundations, 2016). Trust is critical for the effective functioning of the relationship between educator and students. However, this trust can be quickly eradicated when teachers target young Muslims as potential extremists or terrorists. The Prevent strategy, which 'emerged in, fed off, and in turn nourished an expansion in anti-Muslim racism' (Nagdee et al., 2017), is undoubtedly an institutionalised Islamophobic structure. One that needs further interrogation.

Teachers might base decisions about who to report under Prevent either on their enforced or apathetic neutrality or on Prevent training that is 'wholly unsatisfactory' and promotes an 'anti-Muslim bias' (Open Society Foundations, 2016). Prevent operates in a climate of fear fuelled by Islamophobia, which influences educators' pre-determined assumptions and biases about Muslim young people. The implementation of Islamophobic policies has led to some young Muslims, especially those wrongly targeted under Prevent, to 'question their place in British society' (Open Society Foundations, 2016). Consequently, such policies exacerbate the 'them and us' mentality. Perpetuating this othering and exclusion results in the unfair and dangerous labelling of Muslims, influenced by media and political rhetoric, as not being British or not being British enough. To interrogate the Prevent strategy, we must look not only at its effects on the relationship between teacher and student, particularly if young Muslims are erroneously targeted, but also at how labels are casually and wrongly assigned to Muslims as a collective.

Othering, a term created by the cultural theorist Edward W. Said, is a commonly used agenda that seeks to 'other' a minority group on the basis of a culture and beliefs that are fundamentally different from the majority of society. The idea of an alien 'other' reinforces difference and promotes social and political dominance over the 'other'. In his book *Orientalism*, Said writes: 'Orientalism is a study based on the re-thinking of what had for centuries been believed to be an unbridgeable chasm separating East from West.' He suggests that we should 'challenge the notion that difference implies hostility, a frozen reified set of opposed essences, and a whole adversarial knowledge built out of those things' (Said, 2003). Therefore, we must help students fight against labelling and oppression by recognising the media and political influences that fuel negative rhetoric about different communities. Only then can we begin to consider how every student can celebrate their own identity.

As Shirley Steinberg argues, 'the arrogance of whiteness has never waned, nor lost power' (Steinberg, 2017) and through this lens of whiteness there is an ever-present danger of people being 'dismissed as ethnically or racially different' (Modood, 2013). This othering has become a common and damaging form of labelling that seeks to demonise a minority group on the basis of culture and beliefs that are fundamentally different from the norm and are therefore deemed as a threat. This threat might be perceived as a fear among the dominant white majority of losing their control and privilege. The hegemonic strategy of deliberate othering will always reinforce difference and is dependent on the maintenance of whiteness through a form of white supremacy.

The media (including social media) and political rhetoric continuously influence people, including educators. So we need to consider how these narratives inevitably fuel othering. For teachers, the labelling of specific cohorts (for example, Muslim students) can be due to 'personal experience combined with rumour, hearsay and reportage' (Husband et al., 2016), resulting in Muslim communities being labelled 'as "immigrants", "coloureds" or "foreigners"' (Modood, 2013). Racist tropes perpetuated through these generic and degrading labels will reinforce biases but may also lead to young Muslims being reluctant to own and take pride in their identity.

Other students may feel pressured into agreeing to and presenting a form of self-identification through stigmatised and stereotypical constraints of how other people think they should be and behave. For example, Muslim students may believe they should display the identities that have already been decided for them by society. This might be described as a form of 'ethnoracial assignment' (Banks, 2014), a term that refers to socially constructed expectations based solely on a person's ethnicity and race. Jacqueline Stevenson et al. suggest that teachers have 'either stereotypical or overly low expectations of young Muslims' and therefore may (unconsciously) assign certain prerogative labels to their Muslim students (Stevenson et al., 2017). This assimilatory rhetoric can lead to 'imprisoned identities' (Habib, 2017) where young people express how their identity has been predetermined for them by media and political discourses, as well as by wider society, including schooling. This is evident in discourses about belonging and identity, where racialised young people struggle to feel British even if they have been born in Britain and feel that Britain is their home.

Some young people may feel unable to examine their identities in the contexts of schooling and education, particularly as 'students do not often have a chance to explore personal identity intensively in lessons' (Habib, 2017). The significance of education in nurturing future generations must be appreciated, as schools are often the key sites where identities are formed. In her book *The New Folk Devils: Muslim boys and education in England,* Farzana Shain suggests that it is within schools that 'relations of power and dominant cultural definitions are mediated and young people negotiate and contest issues of belonging, citizenship and identity' (Shain, 2011). This particular book is one that I have used in numerous CPD sessions with (mainly white, non-Muslim) teachers as a catalyst for dialogue. We discussed how as a school we could respond sensitively to our students' identities 'by carefully creating culturally diverse spaces where notions of belongings ... can be critically assessed and collaboratively negotiated' (Habib, 2017). However, it is important to consider that identities are always 'multiple, changing, overlapping, and contextual, rather than fixed and static' (Banks, 2014). Identities are also 'inextricably bound up with intersectional experiences that are classed, gendered and racialised' (Habib, 2017). Educators can explore

43

with students the complex interwoven aspects of identities, and how students' identities are fluid and shift according to context and audience, as well as many other factors. Employing features of critical race theory (which will be discussed in more detail in chapter 3) can help teachers to recognise and understand how 'power dynamics of race, class, gender and other social dynamics operate to produce an individual's identity' (Steinberg, 2017).

Some students may feel that their multiple identities are dismissed in schooling and education and tarnished by media and political discourses. Critical pedagogy can provide the tools and praxis (practices) to enable an authentic desire from teachers to respect and celebrate the multiple and evolving identities of all their students.

It may be easier, for some teachers, to embrace student identities that are similar to their own. For example, white, non-Muslim teachers might feel more comfortable teaching white, non-Muslim students, as they appear to be more like themselves. Other teachers may 'adopt a "colour-blind" approach where they pretend not to notice or care about issues of colour or ethnicity' (Arshad, 2012). However, this type of colour-blindness is unhelpful in anti-racist education. Although teachers who claim to 'treat everyone the same' may feel this is a positive stance, it can be a dangerous one to take. Ignoring the colour or ethnicity of our students is actually a form of prejudice and discrimination. As David Gillborn explains, if we treat everyone the same, the dominant and mainstream 'perspectives and interests of white people are constantly enforced over those of minoritised groups' (Gillborn, 2008). Teachers and educators involved in anti-racist work should strive to understand the complexities of their classrooms, and although differences of identities will always exist, there should never be a hierarchy of identity.

CONSCIENTIZAÇÃO

Critical pedagogy gives our students the opportunity to interrogate media and political discourses. It promotes classroom spaces where young people and teachers challenge 'taken-for-granted social truths' and 'struggle for a more just and compassionate moral order capable of sustaining the diversity of life which inhabits our planet' (Simon, 1992).

Critical pedagogy promotes teaching and learning that is linked to the goal of educating our students to commit to the struggle with ongoing relations of power that they see communicated through mainstream media and, sadly, consequently through societal structures.

Critical pedagogy must always remain open and indeterminate. It is not a prescribed method that can be simply applied regardless of context – there is always a genuine possibility. Critical pedagogy is a practice rooted in an ethical-political vision that attempts to take people beyond the world they already believe they know (through media coverage and school and teacher neutrality), but in a way that does not insist on a fixed set of outcomes. A language of possibility can be developed that stimulates student agency and, as described by Freire, a personal *conscientização* (Freire, 1996). *Conscientização* can be translated as a critical consciousness that inspires within our students the bravery, conviction and hope[5] to imagine a different and better world. It gives students the tools to recognise their own place in this world and, importantly, to fulfil the desire to improve their life and the lives of others. Students need the opportunity to struggle for what they believe in, but they also need to know that their teacher is not neutral and is with them every step of the way. As we know, this is often difficult but never impossible.

For authentic critical pedagogy to happen in your classroom and school, your students must know that you support their journey of emancipation and oppose any form of inequality and oppression that they suffer. 'It is important for students to understand how these systems work, why they're in place, and whose interests they protect' (Simon, 1992). Teachers should never embrace neutrality. To be neutral can be perceived by students as a lack of engagement and a lack of interest in current affairs that directly affect them. Educators should never stay silent by being non-committal or choosing not to discuss important matters. According to Freire, 'Washing one's hands of the conflict between the powerful and the powerless means to side with the powerful' (Freire, 1985). The 'powerless' are the very young people that teachers are meant to educate, inspire and have a duty of care for.

---

5   As hope 'grows from commitment to responsibility' (Simon, 1992).

SUGGESTIONS

Interrogate media discourses with your students. You can watch news clips and read articles *with* students, not for them. Students can consider important questions about agenda-setting in the media, such as: why is this story featured in the news? What other opinions about this news story do we need to hear? Why are some current affairs not in the news? How does this news story make you feel? What do you think we should do about this news story? This is one very simple strategy to aid students' acquisition of agency and at the same time show them that you are genuinely interested in these situations. Moreover, you emphasise that as a 'transformative intellectual' (McLaren, 1995) you are unwilling to stay silent about misrepresentation, biased reporting and overt racism in the mainstream media.

Ideally, you want your students to bring you news stories from various media sources for you to collectively analyse in the quest to understand global challenges. Many students will not consume what may be regarded – by their teachers – as mainstream media, which is 'a clear reflection of the postmodern era and the power of new media where we can all connect on a local and global level, building support networks and communities' (Coles & Hassan, 2017). Perhaps you might incorporate regular current affairs quizzes, debates and reading of news reports into your school strategies, and help students to set up social action and awareness groups. Such strategies could be linked to charities that the students wish the school to support when fundraising.

The following suggestions are specifically for educators who teach Muslim students. Teachers need to work alongside their students to interrogate mainstream media labelling. Examine news websites and newspapers to explore the representation (or misrepresentation) of Muslims. Dissect the language that is used in reporting on specific events and particular people. Study how famous Muslims are discussed in the media, such as Riz Ahmed, Bella Hadid, DJ Khaled, Rita Ora, Mohamed Salah, Moeen Ali, Dua Lipa, Guz Khan, Nadiya Hussain and Big Zuu, to name but a few. Does their celebrity status mean they are seen differently from non-celebrity Muslims? Explore how the words 'religion', 'race' and 'ethnicity' are seemingly interchangeable depending on the rhetoric employed. Investigate how Muslims are represented in the media, either via quantitative studies (counting recurring adjectives, for example) or by encouraging dialogues between students. Analyse the complex relationship between identity and Britishness (Habib, 2017). What does it mean to be British? Why are some Muslims represented as more British than others? Is Britishness equated with whiteness?

Allow opportunities for your Muslim students to create poems, stories, performances and art to present their multiple and diverse identities. A powerful way to celebrate identity is through visual stimuli in your classroom and school. Posters and photos can show Muslim students how the school seeks to tackle racism and Islamophobia, as well as how the school admires and respects multiple identities. Break down the stereotypes that students may think you subscribe to, or that students may apply to each other. When critiquing the negative labelling of Muslims students, validate the idea that identities shift, change and are adaptable. Give students opportunities to challenge mainstream myths about Muslim youth. Explore how the Muslim world has given us many innovations, inventions and influences that we take for granted in daily life. These simple suggestions allow teachers to begin to rethink the idea of 'fundamental British values' (Department for Education, 2014), replacing it with opportunities for young people to explore identities, diversities and belonging.

Set up working parties and focus groups for students to discuss relevant current affairs with you as their teacher. Invite them to talk to you about which recent news stories have affected them. Discuss issues of media representation and misrepresentation. Allow students to share their thoughts and feelings with you; to speak their truth uncontaminated by the teacher-student hierarchy.

Take time out of your lessons (or plan time into your schemes of work) to discuss relevant and poignant news coverage within your subject. This may be a lot easier for subjects such as science, RE, English, history and geography, but be creative. Using your authority to stop what you are teaching and to discuss something relevant that has been in the news (or not) is a sure-fire way to step away from being neutral. If we empower students to talk about things that are important to them, we are in the authentic realm of critical pedagogy.

CHAPTER 2
TEACHING

A story in a national teaching publication suggests that 'all teachers should embrace direct instruction' (Ward, 2018). According to the US-based National Institute for Direct Instruction, this is a model for teaching that focuses on 'small learning increments and clearly defined and prescribed teaching tasks'.[6] The creators of the model, Siegfried Engelmann and Wesley Becker, believe that direct instruction can 'improve academic performance as well as certain affective behaviors'. This didactic and authoritative form of teaching is increasingly promoted in English secondary schools, even though direct instruction 'threatens to exacerbate an achievement gap that limits the academic and vocational opportunities for students already burdened by poverty and discrimination' (Eppley & Dudley-Marling, 2019). Paulo Freire describes the transfer of knowledge from the mind of the teacher to the mind of the student, promoted by direct instruction, as the 'banking' model of education (Freire, 1996). He likens teachers who follow this method to bank clerks, depositing selected amounts of prescribed information into students.

The banking approach means that student minds are filled with content and narration – content that is often detached from reality and context. Knowledge should never be seen as a commodity that can be simply transferred from one place to another. In the banking concept of education, knowledge is often seen as a 'gift bestowed by those who consider themselves knowledgeable upon those whom they consider to know nothing' (Freire, 1996). This knowledge therefore becomes hollow,

---

6   www.nifdi.org/what-is-di/basic-philosophy.html

devoid of meaning and, significantly, alienating and oppressive. For the banking concept to work in a classroom there must be an enforced uniformity, a focus on the outward appearance of attention, decorum and obedience, and a reliance upon student passivity and receptivity. When a culture of conformity is promoted, it ultimately leads to passive absorption of knowledge. Students are simply consuming knowledge rather than actively transforming it.

Freire declares that this form of teaching is based on an 'ideology of oppression' (Freire, 1996) where classrooms present and advocate only dominant narratives to students. If only certain prepotent[7] narratives are deliberately heard, while other voices are consciously silenced, students only ever experience dominant knowledge that represents the 'authority'. This authority is sometimes referred to as the hegemony, meaning the dominance of one social group over another. Hegemonic control is often exercised subtly through cultural means and economic power. As Basil Bernstein suggests, a dominant and hegemonic narrative pervades schools and education via sociolinguistic codes (Bernstein, 1971). White, Christian, middle-class codes – of language, values and culture – are afforded to students of all ethnicities, religions and classes. The teaching of hegemonic knowledge relies on a pedagogy of consent and coercion, and the most effective pedagogy for this is direct instruction. 'The selective organization, transmission and evaluation of knowledge is intimately bound up with patterns of authority and control' (Bernstein, 1971). The transmission of hegemonic knowledge through an authoritative pedagogy produces a stagnant social structure; a form of cultural production. Pierre Bourdieu describes this form of pedagogy as 'the most effective means of perpetuating the existing social pattern', as it 'provides an apparent justification for social inequalities' (Bourdieu, 1974). As Marxists would argue, this form of education legitimises and reproduces class inequalities (of dominance and subordination). In essence, the education that the dominant classes offer to the working class is the education that maintains the working class. And as Freire declares, 'it would be extremely naive to expect the dominant classes to develop a type of education that would enable subordinate classes to perceive social injustices critically' (Freire, 1985).

---

7   Meaning greater than others in power or influence.

Through a pedagogy of oppression, the experiences, histories, cultures and narratives of students are deliberately ignored and devalued and replaced with the blind consumption of hegemonic chosen knowledge. Through this traditional form of teaching, students are mere spectators in their own learning.

EDUCATIONAL WISDOM

Teacher recruitment and retention in England (and other countries) is in crisis. A 2023 survey of school leaders by the NAHT found that 57% would not recommend school leadership as a career choice, and almost one in two school leaders had felt a need for mental health or wellbeing support in the previous year. The report claimed that the 'failure of the Department for Education's 2019 recruitment and retention strategy to address the key drivers of the leadership supply crisis has come home to roost' (NAHT, 2023). Schools are therefore hastily promoting an increased number of inexperienced teachers into leadership roles. Thus, fewer and fewer teachers are spending years in the classroom honing a form of educational wisdom.

This educational wisdom is not a skill or competence, or a result of regurgitating fashionable cognitive research into a school, but a quality that permeates and characterises the whole person. Teachers no longer spend a substantial amount of time in their classrooms with their students. The beautiful, career-long study of the art of teaching is no longer seen as necessary, nor desirable. Schools are looking for quick, basic modes of teaching. Off-the-shelf strategies are sought after, leading teachers to follow a prescribed and often simplistic way for everyone to teach. As well as being financially lucrative for their creators, these strategies intentionally deskill the teacher. And, importantly, they coerce teachers into a neutral, apolitical method of teaching. Novice practitioners are asked to dutifully follow simple routines that impart selected knowledge from teacher to student.

In 1911, Frederick Winslow Taylor, an American mechanical engineer, published a book called *The Principles of Scientific Management*, which proposed that by standardising labour and simplifying jobs, productivity would increase. Taylor's theory eliminated the need for skilled work by delegating each employee one simple routine. But, 'although this method increased the productivity of factories, it stripped employees their freedom to choose their work, as well as how it should be done' (Ireh, 2016). Taylor's ideas have continued to influence education, both in the US and in the UK. Wayne Au suggests that the 'new Taylorism' has ensured that 'teachers' classroom practises are increasingly standardized by high-stakes testing ... and pre-packaged, corporate curricula aimed specifically at teaching to the tests' (Au, 2011). Even though evidence of Taylorism has largely vanished in the industrial workplace, 'schools are still largely driven by conceptions of teaching and learning that have their roots in Taylorism or what is often described as the "factory model" of schooling' (Ross, 2010).

Traditional forms of pedagogy such as direct instruction, where 'knowledge is transmitted in a context where the teacher has maximal control or surveillance' (Bernstein, 1971), restrict the kind of learning that takes place. This deliberately ensures that only carefully selected and 'legitimate' knowledge emerges in the classroom. Direct instruction focuses on how to teach students (as objects) in a specific approach and how students can learn in a definitive way. This ultimately affects how students are taught. Through the banking model of teaching, students are trained via a non-negotiable structure to passively receive regular deposits of stagnant knowledge. Therefore, a prescribed style of teaching is necessary.

TEACH LIKE A CHAMPION

Teachers now often learn their trade via an over-reliance on unsophisticated 'teaching by numbers' manuals. This is akin to painting by numbers, where novice artists are told where on the canvas to paint, in what order and in which colour. These instructions are counter to any real search for educational wisdom. The art and craft of teaching and learning are constricted – and often ignored – in preference for didactic behavioural drills. 'When teachers learn only the techniques, they never question their "why" of teaching' (McNutt, 2021). The most notable example of these popular identikit-teaching guides is Doug Lemov's *Teach Like a Champion* (2010, 2015, 2021).

Lemov founded the US-based Uncommon Schools, which 'forged a reputation for its work in starting and managing urban schools with the primary aim of raising aspirations and improving opportunities among low income students in more than 50 schools across the North-East states' (Morrison, 2020). All teachers at Uncommon Schools use the *Teach Like a Champion* model. According to Ian Cushing, 'teachers are constructed as "coaches", "heroes", "elites" and, indeed, "champions" who are engaged in philanthropic and life-affirming work, as neocolonial missionaries whose job is to save poor, "urban" children' (Cushing, 2021). The *Teach Like a Champion* approach is becoming increasingly prominent in English secondary schools and is heavily promoted by politicians and education policymakers: Lemov's ideology has had 'considerable influence in UK education' (Cushing, 2021), 'winning praise from former schools minister Nick Gibb' (Staufenberg, 2021).

The Department for Education (2016) recommends that teachers subscribe to Lemov's approach. According to Cushing, it serves 'the interests of the DfE in the delivery of their macro-level policies on behaviour management as a cheap, ready-made, quick-fix manual for teachers' (Cushing, 2021). The UK government's 'behaviour tsar', Tom Bennett, who leads the DfE's behaviour hubs project, is a prominent supporter of *Teach Like a Champion*, writing: 'Great innovators such as Doug Lemov have shown in his Uncommon Schools that clear routines and a shared collective understanding of the school's community norms can lead to enormous gains in outcomes' (Bennett, 2017). Cushing writes that Lemov's handbook is 'a regular reference point as "research-informed" practice by the founder of ResearchED, Tom Bennett', and *Teach Like a Champion* is also 'highly valued by Teach First (a UK-based teacher education programme), with trainee teachers instructed on its mechanisms during their 5-week training programme, in which they are exposed to a neoliberal education ideology based on strict discipline and meritocracy' (Cushing, 2021). The DfE's 'How Pupils Learn' exemplar materials for early career teachers refer to Teach First as an example of good practice (Department for Education, 2022b). Schools and trusts are buying (quite literally) into these strategies, as school leaders see them as uncomplicated for insufficiently trained teachers, easy to replicate and simple to quality-assure.

According to Chris McNutt, executive director of the Human Restoration Project, the techniques in *Teach Like a Champion* 'are heavily based off the work of radical behaviorism founder, B.F. Skinner. Most well known for the "Skinner Box", a lever that animals would pull to be positively rewarded for simple tasks' (McNutt, 2021). The advocated strategies promote 'behavioural norms through a pedagogy of order, uniformity, and obedience' (Treuhaft-Ali, 2016). McNutt suggests that these techniques 'mirror military boot camps' with 'an extreme focus on respect, unquestioning authority, and controlling movement' (McNutt, 2021). Layla Treuhaft-Ali suggests that 'Lemov positions himself as an objective, non-ideological observer above the fray of political debate' (Treuhaft-Ali, 2016). However, when a whole-school teaching approach is based on behaviorism, it is political. As discussed in chapter 1, 'in the same way that remaining neutral is a political act, remaining neutral and objective toward rote teaching materials is a political act' (McNutt, 2021). When *Teach Like a Champion* recommends highly disciplined and authoritative teaching, it limits any capacity for students to become critically aware or politically responsible. A student who is taught through this approach will be subject to an authoritarian conception of teaching. Classrooms and learning will be centred around complete control, with certain students seen as deficient. Further analysis of which students are seen as behaviourally deficient is necessary.

A critical point that is often ignored or overlooked in discussions about the appropriate use of *Teach Like a Champion* strategies in England's secondary schools is that 'nearly all Uncommon students are Black or Hispanic (94%)' (Uncommon Schools, 2019). The *Teach Like a Champion* pedagogical theory is carefully selected and steers the educational process towards the production of predetermined learning behaviours but also predetermined identities. In the 2015 edition of Lemov's book, 'negative assertions were made about students of Color and their ability to succeed in the classroom based upon their race … He characterized behavior and language as deficit by describing them as both unscholarly and an impediment to classroom culture' (Valenti, 2019). According to Cushing, there are 'highly regulated attempts to make students think, act and talk in accordance with white, middle-class behaviours' (Cushing, 2021). 'Lemov promoted the assumption that academic disparities between

White students and students of Color can be remedied by altering, or fixing, perceived student deficiencies' (Valenti, 2019).

In essence, this form of education is now a 'planned enculturation' (Osberg & Biesta, 2008). Enculturation is the process by which people are taught the values and behaviours deemed appropriate or necessary for them to succeed. Kayla Stewart Valenti, who analysed *Teach Like a Champion 2.0* (2015) through the lens of critical race theory, found 'evidence of racially coded language and terminology that attributes deficient characteristics to students of Color', as well as examples of 'language that promotes dominant ideology, further preserving White supremacy within schooling' (Valenti, 2019). Lemov focuses on 'theories of discipline which place responsibility on individuals to change themselves, rather than attempting to address structural inequalities at the intersection points of language, poverty and race' (Cushing, 2021).

The *Teach Like a Champion* model has the power to develop the sustained and permanent enculturation of our students, specifically our marginalised students. 'Lemov's use of racially coded language [is] rooted in cultural deficiency, and terminology that perpetuates dominant ideology ... techniques which advocate for the socialization and assimilation of certain student behaviors' (Valenti, 2019). Any attempt to place limits on the kinds of natural identities and meanings that emerge in a classroom is an attempt to ensure that students learn 'legitimately' and in 'the correct way'; failure among students to adapt to this way of learning, or opposition to these methods, is perceived as educational failure. 'Imposing sanctions for relatively trivial offences – a cornerstone of [the 'no excuses' culture] – pushes more students into a disciplinary system,' writes the journalist Nick Morrison, adding, 'It is not too hard to see the enthusiastic embrace of no excuses in some quarters in the UK as responsible for doubling the rate of school exclusions over the last six years' (Morrison, 2020). In 2020, Uncommon Schools, 'known for their uncompromising approach to student behavior' (Morrison, 2020), published a letter on its website (since removed) 'apologising to students and staff who had suffered traumatic experiences at the hands of their policies' (Cushing, 2021). This U-turn was supported by many educationalists but was also 'met with dismay from many UK supporters of the [*Teach Like a Champion*] industry' (Cushing, 2021).

Teachers should never have preconceived assumptions about what their students can achieve. They should not attempt to initiate or socialise students into a common way of being and should never try to make students more similar or progress in the 'correct way'. Teachers should allow students to be educated without a predetermined idea of what embodies success. The approaches in *Teach Like a Champion* prevent any genuine attempt to develop students' personal and unique distinctness. Lemov encourages '"champion" teachers to advance student outcomes by rejecting components of a student's cultural identity' (Valenti, 2019). Teachers should never ignore or devalue individual student identities, nor try to socialise people into a particular way of being. Rather, educators must maintain a 'logic of emergence'[8] (Osberg, 2005) to allow students to grow and develop as individuals. Learning must be centred around the experiences, contexts, cultures and histories of the students in a particular school, in order to empower them. The *Teach Like a Champion* ideology 'takes agency away from teachers' (Morrison, 2020) and deliberately disables the true role of the educator – to develop the social, intellectual, moral and political minds of young people.

Direct instruction delivered through a pedagogical approach like *Teach Like a Champion* purposely and consciously shapes students into possessing and displaying certain kinds of subjectivities. These indoctrinated habits and behaviours will mean that students can only passively 'fit in' to today's society. In an email discussion between Henry A. Giroux and me on this form of education, he commented: 'If these critics think that knowledge speaks for itself and does not have to connect in some ways to the lives of their students, it is because they don't care about these students and view them as disposable, while treating them as indifferent and dumb.'

Lemov advocates classroom practices based on oppressive disciplinary rules. His strategies should be seen as a right-wing authoritarian pedagogy attempting to subordinate schools, deskill teachers and further oppress marginalised students. This is not education; this is domestication.

---

8   'Educators must try to understand that the only knowledge which they have – about who they are dealing with, and the goal of their teaching – is a product of the emerging situation itself. This knowledge, in other words, is contingent, not static' (Osberg, 2005).

'Lemov is able to promote his pedagogy and race-based techniques under the guise of closing the achievement gap and fixing the effects of poverty without acknowledging the effects of structural racism' (Valenti, 2019). This approach 'serves the interests of the oppressors, who care neither to have the world revealed nor to see it transformed' (Freire, 1996). Through this pedagogy, where learning is never centred around the experiences and contexts of our students, teaching becomes a basic act where the only goal for the classroom is to instil 'a culture of conformity and an insipid, passive absorption of carefully selected knowledge' (Coles, 2014b). Therefore, young people will never be empowered to become critical and engaged agents capable of making a change.

Decisions by schools and multi-academy trusts to base their entire learning culture and ethos on a series of dubiously researched teaching manuals,[9] and the increasing return to a more conservative way of teaching, are unmistakably deliberate. Lemov's oppressive ideology is promoted and celebrated by politicians and education policymakers in the UK, who are said to be 'lapping up his ideas' (Weale, 2014). Sadly, teachers are becoming increasingly non-committal about how to teach, preferring to rely on standard operating procedures in their classrooms; they are regressing to neutral and apolitical positions within their own trade and vocation. In the introduction to the first edition of *Teach Like a Champion* (2010), Lemov declares, 'I am not writing this book to engage in a philosophical debate', and thereby his readers are discouraged from engaging in any meaningful critiques of his pedagogy. As bell hooks writes, 'Given that our educational institutions are so deeply invested in a banking system, teachers are more rewarded when we do not teach against the grain' (hooks, 1994). Opposing the banking model of teaching and an oppressive pedagogy such as *Teach Like a Champion* is now seen as a subversive act, but teaching 'against the grain' is exactly the approach that critical pedagogues must fight for.

---

9   It has been suggested that 'there was no consistent evidence that *Teach Like a Champion* positively impacted student academic achievement or student behavior' (Reed, 2020).

AUTHORITARIANISM

When it comes to student learning, there is a huge difference between learning *from* the teacher and being taught *by* the teacher. A student who is taught by their teacher will be subject to an authoritarian concept of teaching that serves to ensure that students submit to authority. Authority in education can be the teacher's voice, but also the teacher's own thoughts.

If a teacher believes that their students have empty minds that need to be filled, they regard their students' ignorance as absolute, and this belief justifies the teacher's own existence. As soon as 'banking' teachers shake off the narcissistic idea that they must take every opportunity to remind their class how clever they are and how much they know, they start to break down the self-imposed hierarchic barriers between themselves and the students they serve. However, the most positive form of rebuke to authoritarianism is the power of critical thought, challenge and questioning. When a student learns *from* their teacher, they are, in a fundamental sense, in shared control of the learning. The educator forgoes any hierarchical authority for the sake of emancipatory education – an approach that goes beyond the simple transfer of knowledge. Knowledge must be seen as an emergence of meaning. An emergence of what we understand as we participate in the world through individual actions. An emergence that always represents something more real than itself.

Through transformative methods of teaching and learning, students are encouraged to question the dominant structure of socioeconomic and political relations. The transformative teacher will look to the benefits of critical pedagogy, which enable students to think critically about society and thus catalyse 'a desire to challenge the views they are taught' (Coles, 2014b). Teachers should not be trained 'to operate as unresponsive robots that are supposed to intervene on equally unresponsive objects' (Biesta, 2012). Instead, teachers need to engage in educational relationships and encounters to ensure that students become aware of their individual reality by investigating their daily life. Classrooms should be a space where students – with teachers – can agree to demand a different world and to discuss and prepare for alternatives.

TRANSFORMATIVE INTELLECTUALS

Classrooms of student passivity and strict authoritative routines prevent any form of dialogue and collaboration between the teacher and their students. But when students learn *from* their teacher, the student gains a position of agency rather than receptivity or perhaps even gratitude. All teachers have the potential to become a 'transformative intellectual' (McLaren, 1995) through the understanding and teaching of critical pedagogy. This philosophy allows students to be educated (to learn and remember knowledge) and, vitally, to develop a personal *conscientização* (Freire, 1996), which translates from Freire's native language of Brazilian Portuguese as 'critical consciousness'. Critical pedagogy is concerned with students learning knowledge, but also supplementary, often hidden knowledge that will enable them to recognise that many of them inhabit an oppressive system. Through this teaching of reality, students gain an educated awareness of their own place in this system and, importantly, the knowledge to do something about it.

The challenge of teachers becoming 'transformative intellectuals' (McLaren, 1995) rather than 'bankers' relies on them moving away from being technicians of content who simply transmit knowledge. A transformative teacher using critical pedagogy can be an essential helping hand and an informed guide on the pathway of emancipation for the students they teach. In an interview, Giroux said, 'critical pedagogy must be seen as a political and moral project and not a technique. Pedagogy is always political because it is connected to the acquisition of agency. As a political project, critical pedagogy illuminates the relationships among knowledge, authority, and power" (Babiak, 2006). To become transformative teachers, we must move away from being neutral content providers who simply transmit apolitical, hegemonic and oppressive knowledge. Teachers must embrace critical pedagogy and learn to be committed, political and willing to teach against the grain.

When an educator is teaching against the grain, they are honing the skills and motivation required to become a transformative teacher and constantly critique oppressive ideologies such as Engelmann's direct instruction and Lemov's *Teach Like a Champion*. Through this conservative education, democracy is replaced by conformity, political illiteracy and often (though the selection of knowledge) a deliberate historical amnesia. Democracy will only be successful if students are allowed to be curious about the past, challenge societal authority, critique inequalities and be hopeful for the future. The teacher deploying critical pedagogy will work relentlessly to nurture a generation of students who develop an educated mistrust of every myth and falsehood that has been indoctrinated before. By shielding our students from the embedded and systemic structures of power, no matter if we do it protectively, we prevent them from following their own paths of self-emancipation. Students need to develop a critical consciousness about historical and current injustices before they develop the mechanisms to change society and ultimately improve their situation. This is the goal of democracy. This is the goal of education.

SUGGESTIONS

The transformative teacher will enable their students to develop the tools required to explore social justice, their self and their society (Habib, 2017). The transformative teacher will encourage and promote reflective encounters about historical oppression and a critical consciousness about social change. When teachers explore identity and societal issues with young people, the classroom becomes a space where learning and teaching is *done together* by both teacher and students.

The transformative teacher will unearth their own prejudices and biases in order to become a morally effective educator who responds to the politics of our time. They will be passionate about the liberatory powers of education, and reflective and critical about their own pedagogies, practices and philosophies. The transformative teacher creates spaces where all students can collaboratively explore how society works. Students will have opportunities to safely discuss and challenge political myths, deep-rooted racist structures and oppressive ideologies.

The transformative teacher inhabits an education that values the concepts of: collaboration as a respectful and caring dialogue; praxis, moving beyond theoretical reflection and critical dialogue into reflexive action; and *conscientização* as a critical consciousness of oppression. All this is necessary to educate and liberate marginalised communities. The pedagogy of possibility and liberation is essential to provide opportunities for students to critique the social world, with the ultimate goal of working to transform and improve their own lives and the society they live in.

However, teachers themselves also require the right tools and attributes. Richard D. Sawyer argues that it is 'easy to speak of teaching in ways that respect' democracy, inclusion and agency, but in practice 'it is exceptionally difficult to do so' (Sawyer, 2016). Critical pedagogy is not a prescribed technique that should be applied loosely to any and every situation. The transformative teacher must be aware of and sensitive to the context of their school and their students.

Exploring identities is an important feature of transformational education and a key tenet of critical race theory. If an educator isn't aware of the diverse identities in their classroom, how can they expect to develop relationships with their students and become morally effective teachers? If diverse identities are ignored or disrespected then only the teacher's identity will surface, resulting in the assertion of a hegemonic narrative. This can perpetuate a sense of white superiority in the classroom. As discussed in chapter 1, a symbiotic relationship is necessary for critical pedagogy to be successful and transformational, one where the students understand the teacher's modus operandi, and where teachers know and value their students' identities. As educators, we need to work hard to learn about the cultural, religious, ethnic and class heritages of young people and their communities. By building these authentic relationships, teachers can begin to understand, respect and celebrate the identities of their students.

Most English secondary schools will follow the national curriculum. The content prescribed in these documents is ultimately the knowledge that students will be assessed on in their internal and external examinations. It is vital to clarify that critical pedagogy never sacrifices the essential subject knowledge that students need in order to succeed in their exams. The transformative teacher, using critical pedagogy principles, will teach essential content as well as help their students to learn supplementary and additional knowledge that allows them to interrogate and critique society and their place within it.

On the following pages are excerpts from national curriculum specifications from several subjects, alongside suggestions and questions for subject teachers to consider in order to successfully implement critical pedagogy approaches in their classrooms.

ART

From the key stage 3 programme of study: 'Pupils should be taught: about the history of art, craft, design and architecture, including periods, styles and major movements from ancient times up to the present day.'[10]

- Which artists do you explore in your classroom?
- Is this your decision?
- Is your decision based on your accumulated resources and the fact that you have taught these artists before?
- Which artists do your students want to explore? How do you know?
- How are the artists that students learn about presented in your teaching?
- Are certain forms of art considered more important than others?
- Have you considered seeking contributions from an artist in residence with a similar background to your students?

---

10 www.gov.uk/government/publications/national-curriculum-in-england-art-and-design-programmes-of-study/national-curriculum-in-england-art-and-design-programmes-of-study#key-stage-3

BUSINESS

From the GCSE subject content: 'GCSE specifications in business must require students to apply their knowledge and understanding to business decision making. This includes: how different business contexts affect business decisions.'[11]

- Do you explore which businesses and charities receive government backing?
- Why are some businesses seen as more morally credible than others?
- Do you reference companies that have been accused of not paying enough tax in the UK based on the size of the business, such as Amazon, Starbucks, Google, Apple, eBay and Facebook?

CITIZENSHIP

From the secondary national curriculum: 'The national curriculum for citizenship aims to ensure that all pupils: are equipped with the skills to think critically and debate political questions, to enable them to manage their money on a day-to-day basis, and plan for future financial needs.'[12]

- Can your students debate political questions in your lessons?
- How do you teach your students to be informed?
- How do you teach your students to be articulate?
- Which political questions do you explore?
- Do you encourage your students to be social agents?
- Which charities does your school fundraise for? Why these charities?
- Have you considered asking your students which charities they would like to support?

11 assets.publishing.service.gov.uk/government/uploads/system/uploads/attachment_data/file/485407/Business_GCSE.pdf

12 assets.publishing.service.gov.uk/government/uploads/system/uploads/attachment_data/file/840002/Secondary_national_curriculum_corrected_PDF.pdf

DESIGN AND TECHNOLOGY

From the KS3 programme of study: 'When designing and making, pupils should be taught to: use research and exploration, such as the study of different cultures, to identify and understand user needs.'[13]

- Which designers do you explore? Is this your decision?
- Which designers do your students want to explore? How do you know?
- Which designers are seen to be the most important?
- Do all designers receive equal merit?
- Have you explored why some designers are seen as more morally credible than others?

ENGLISH

From the KS3 programme of study: 'The national curriculum for English aims to ensure that all pupils: appreciate our rich and varied literary heritage.'[14]

- Have you considered how you define 'our' rich and varied literary heritage?
- Which books/texts do you explore in KS3?
- Which books do you offer in your library and on your reading lists?
- Have you considered that 'only 2% of GCSE students study a book written by a female author' (Hall, 2023)?
- Have you considered that many books studied in English 'were written at points in history when social narratives were mainly limited to the perspectives of straight white men' (Boakye, 2022)?

---

13 assets.publishing.service.gov.uk/government/uploads/system/uploads/attachment_data/file/239089/SECONDARY_national_curriculum_-_Design_and_technology.pdf

14 assets.publishing.service.gov.uk/government/uploads/system/uploads/attachment_data/file/244215/SECONDARY_national_curriculum_-_English2.pdf

'The national curriculum for English aims to ensure that all pupils: are competent in the arts of speaking and listening, making formal presentations, demonstrating to others and participating in debate.'[8]

- How do you use these opportunities for students to 'speak up and shout out'?
- What do you debate?
- Who decides the subjects of debates?
- How do you ensure that debates happen in safe spaces?
- As a teacher, how do you react to your students' opinions?
- Have you considered the amount of time you spend talking during class debates? What will your role be?

GEOGRAPHY

From the KS3 programme of study: 'Pupils should be taught to understand, through the use of detailed place-based exemplars at a variety of scales, the key processes in human geography relating to: population and urbanisation; international development; economic activity in the primary, secondary, tertiary and quaternary sectors; and the use of natural resources.'[15]

From the GCSE subject content: 'GCSE specifications in geography should enable students to build on their key stage 3 knowledge and skills to: gain understanding of the interactions between people and environments, change in places and processes over space and time, and the interrelationship between geographical phenomena at different scales and in different contexts.'[16]

- Do you discuss genocides recognised by the international community and courts or individual states – e.g. Cambodia, Armenia, Namibia, Rwanda, Srebrenica, Sudan, Palestine, Yazidis in Iraq, Rohingya in Myanmar, Uyghurs in China?

---

15   assets.publishing.service.gov.uk/government/uploads/system/uploads/attachment_data/file/239087/SECONDARY_national_curriculum_-_Geography.pdf
16   assets.publishing.service.gov.uk/government/uploads/system/uploads/attachment_data/file/301253/GCSE_geography.pdf

CRITICAL PEDAGOGY: A TEACHER'S COMPANION

- Do you discuss the rule and effects of the British Empire?
- Do you discuss the partitioning of India?
- From which perspective do you discuss migration?

HISTORY

From the GCSE subject content: 'GCSE specifications in history should enable students to: develop the ability to ask relevant questions about the past, to investigate issues critically and to make valid historical claims by using a range of sources in their historical context; develop an awareness of why people, events and developments have been accorded historical significance and how and why different interpretations have been constructed about them.'[17]

- Do you allow your students to think critically?
- Which history do you explore and why?
- Which narratives and viewpoints do you consider in your lessons?
- Do you explore the 'whitewashing' of history?
- Are you aware that a GCSE textbook was pulled after 'claims that it had "whitewashed" Jewish history' (Turner, 2020)?
- Are you aware that 'Black history is not currently a mandatory part of the national curriculum' (Thompson, 2020)?
- Do you agree or disagree that history teaching can be 'just another manifestation of the ugly revisionism practised in the recounting of Britain's bloody history' (Lais, 2017)?

---

17 assets.publishing.service.gov.uk/government/uploads/system/uploads/ attachment_data/file/310549/history_GCSE_formatted.pdf

MUSIC

From the KS3 programme of study: 'Pupils should be taught to: develop a deepening understanding of the music that they perform and to which they listen, and its history.'[18]

- Which musical genres do you explore?
- Which musical genres and musicians do your students want to explore?
- How do you feel when you read that 'the teaching of music can be white-washed' (Robbins, 2018)?
- Do you explore how political consciousness and social movements can be taught through forms of music such as folk, blues, reggae, punk and hip hop?

PSHE

From the government's PSHE guidance: 'Teachers are best placed to understand the needs of their pupils and do not need additional central prescription.'[19]

- As a teacher of PSHE, what are you going to teach in this essential subject?
- And, vitally, how are you going to teach it?

---

18 www.gov.uk/government/publications/national-curriculum-in-england-music-programmes-of-study/national-curriculum-in-england-music-programmes-of-study#key-stage-3

19 www.gov.uk/government/publications/personal-social-health-and-economic-education-pshe/personal-social-health-and-economic-pshe-education#personal-social-health-and-economic-education

SCIENCE

From the KS3 programme of study: 'Pupils should be taught about: the production of carbon dioxide by human activity and the impact on climate.'[20]

- Do you discuss why people and organisations have different views on climate change?
- Do you discuss the international perspectives of climate change and global warming?
- What are your views on the government supporting schools and teachers 'to deliver world-leading climate change education through a model science curriculum, which will be in place by 2023' (Department for Education, 2021).

From the KS4 programme of study: 'Students should be taught about: carbon compounds, both as fuels and feedstock, and the competing demands for limited resources.'[21]

- Do you discuss how the demand for raw materials has effects across the world?
- Do you consider that the 'sum total of the political effects generated by the oil industry makes oil a leading cause of war' (Colgan, 2013)?
- Do you discuss the historical impact of the demand for raw materials from colonies across the British Empire?

---

20 assets.publishing.service.gov.uk/government/uploads/system/uploads/attachment_data/file/335174/SECONDARY_national_curriculum_-_Science_220714.pdf

21 www.gov.uk/government/publications/national-curriculum-in-england-science-programmes-of-study/national-curriculum-in-england-science-programmes-of-study#key-stage-4

CHAPTER 3
NARRATIVES

> *Theresa May, where's the money for Grenfell?*
> *What, you think we just forgot about Grenfell?*
> *You criminals, and you got the cheek to call us savages.*
> *You should do some jail time, you should pay some damages,*
> *We should burn your house down and see if you can manage this.*
> **Reproduced with kind permission from Stormzy**

In a live performance at the 2018 Brit Awards, the grime artist Stormzy spoke out against Theresa May, the prime minister at the time, and her apparent mishandling of the Grenfell tragedy. In June 2017, 72 people died after a fire broke out in the 24-storey Grenfell Tower in West London. Many music fans (including me) and social commentators saw Stormzy's political critique as an iconic moment in recent pop history; others didn't. One tabloid spokesperson who lambasted Stormzy was Amanda Platell, an Australian journalist who writes for the *Daily Mail*. Platell accused Stormzy of ingratitude for vocally opposing the government: 'For all his life Stormzy has happily benefited from the health care, housing and education opportunities the government, whether Tory or Labour, has provided … is it asking too much that he show a scintilla of gratitude to the country that offered his mother and him so much? Instead of trashing it' (Platell, 2018). Her criticism didn't focus on what Stormzy said, or on how or where he chose to say it, but rather on the fact that someone *like* Stormzy could or indeed should say such a thing. According to Kristel Tracey, Platell's article 'screams "You are here because we allowed you to be – not because you had any right to be"' (Tracey, 2018). The implication was that a Black British man did not have the right or the legitimacy to comment on social or political issues in the country of his birth.

TO BE AN UNDERSTUDY IN YOUR OWN STORY

Black voices are often not heard. As Quinn McKew writes, 'One of the darkest legacies of racism in America is the near-complete removal of black voices from issues of consequence ... Only when we stop and listen, when people are *heard*, do we begin to break down the barriers of inequality' (McKew, 2020). Heidi Mirza describes how Black British people, particularly women, 'are both visible and invisible' (Membis, 2011). Mirza highlights that many are perceived as 'mute visible objects'; they are seen but not heard (Mirza, 2015). Muslim students in higher education can also find it difficult to 'express their views and opinions' (Ghani & Nagdee, 2018). Sughra Ahmed reports that 'much is written about young Muslims but we rarely seem to actually hear their voices' (Ahmed, 2009). Whenever a societal issue arises that concerns minority groups, there is never a shortage of so-called 'experts' commenting via mainstream media. Predominantly it is white males who are given the media platform to talk about these situations, while the voices of those who are directly affected by the issues are seldom heard or allowed to be heard; relevant and authentic opinions are excluded from the conversations. Ghena Krayem, a Muslim woman, describes what it is like 'to be the understudy in your own story, to be relegated to the wings of life's stage while others say your lines for you' (Krayem, 2018). This chapter, therefore, focuses on why white – and usually male – dominant narratives are commonly seen as important, correct and mainstream, and why more diverse narratives are often criticised, silenced and ignored. We will discuss how critical pedagogy can always ensure that our Black, Asian and minority ethnic[22] students are never understudies in their own stories.

---

22 I am not comfortable using this term to describe individuals and communities that fall outside the frequently used 'white British/white other' ethnic categories. Here, the term clarifies the typically marginalised and minoritised students I am referring to. However, I am very much aware of the importance of referencing individuals in a more nuanced way. I would encourage the reader to investigate this complex area, visiting www.nhsrho.org/news/survey-finds-bame-bme-and-ethnic-minority-not-representative as a starting point.

WHITE PRIVILEGE

The criticism faced by Stormzy when he challenged the government's handling of Grenfell revealed a pervasive narrative where 'brown and black Britons have little legitimate claim to this country' (Tracey, 2018). It becomes difficult for certain voices to offer social commentary, and controversial for these commentators to question government decisions that perpetuate social injustice – the very issues that may directly affect those who are being silenced and criticised. However, other voices are heard loudly, and those that are commonly afforded attention in the mainstream media often make use of their white privilege. In the case of Platell, 'whiteness apparently gives her the inherent right to question Stormzy's British credentials' (Tracey, 2018).

White privilege can be described as a socially constructed entitlement of racial power where white people benefit from unseen and unconscious advantages that are denied to people of colour in identical situations (Delgado & Stefancic, 2012). Peggy McIntosh lists the many privileges that white people enjoy, rely on and benefit from, including: 'I can turn on the television or open to the front page of the paper and see people of my race widely represented', 'I can be sure that my children will be given curricular materials that testify to the existence of their race' and 'I do not have to educate my children to be aware of systemic racism for their own daily physical protection' (McIntosh, 1989). Another of these privileges is 'I can criticize our government and talk about how much I fear its policies and behavior without being seen as a cultural outsider'. This privilege is not readily available to marginalised and minoritised people, as exemplified by Platell's criticism of Stormzy. By understanding the role of whiteness as a power structure, we begin to contemplate that this creates and reinforces a hierarchy of narratives. Sadly, this can be witnessed in the classroom and school setting.

As discussed in chapter 1, the role of the teacher is becoming increasingly depoliticised. In 2021, Nadhim Zahawi, then the education secretary, told schools that they 'should not teach contested theories and opinions as fact', including 'contested views about "white privilege"' (Whittaker, 2021). The Department for Education's guidance on political impartiality in schools states that teachers 'can of course teach about partisan political views and explore them with pupils. This will be an important part of teaching about many historical and political issues' (Department for Education, n.d.). The documentation directs teachers to 'offer a balanced presentation of opposing views … this doesn't mean that different views are always given equal time in teaching or cannot be critically assessed'. The DfE encourages teachers to 'challenge misinformation and extreme views, such as those based on discrimination and prejudice'. The political teacher, deploying critical pedagogy in their classroom, must agree that critically analysing dominant narratives and exploring counter-narratives is exactly what the DfE guidance recommends.

COUNTER-NARRATIVES

Exploring counter-narratives with students will lead to an informed resistance to the dominant and hegemonic narratives they often hear. This can and will result in students gaining a sense of agency. Teachers must encourage 'forms of counterdiscourse with which to challenge existing forms of ideological hegemony' (Simon, 1992). Critical pedagogy guides students to understand how mainstream and dominant narratives work and, importantly, how counter-narratives can act as an antidote to authoritarianism.

Encouraging students to become informed, politically literate citizens is one of the goals of critical pedagogy. However, schools will often carefully monitor certain political views and humanitarian activism to ensure that counter-narratives are silenced. At an East London primary school, an eight-year-old child, Yahya, whose mother is from Gaza, 'was disciplined for wearing a Palestine flag on his jacket' (Kimber, 2023). Another incident made national headlines after a Muslim teenager in Luton 'wore a "Free Palestine" badge to school' and 'asked for permission to fundraise for children affected by the Israeli occupation' (*The Independent*, 2016). This act of civic courage and political awareness from a young person was not encouraged or celebrated, but instead criminalised. The boy's teachers 'referred him to police under Prevent – the controversial government anti-radicalisation programme, which critics have claimed is heavy-handed, discriminatory and ineffective' (*The Independent*, 2016). A report from Rights Watch UK suggests that targeting Muslim children via the Prevent strategy, 'making them feel that they are not welcome to discuss political or religious matters at school, and creating a dynamic in which Muslim youth come to be fearful of the educational setting and distrustful of their teachers and their classmates, is counter-productive, discriminatory, and a violation of the fundamental rights that are at the heart of the very civil society the government seeks to protect' (Rights Watch UK, 2016). A school that I once worked in did not wish to encourage students to support a Syrian humanitarian charity for fear of receiving unwanted attention from Ofsted. Censorship of any form of moral agency from students sends a powerful message that certain political and humanitarian causes should not be supported.

There is a stark disparity between the ways that schools have responded to the tragic loss of lives in Ukraine and in Palestine. A 2022 survey of 532 UK primary schools, secondary schools, sixth forms and universities highlighted this double standard. According to the survey, which was undertaken by the advocacy group CAGE International, '96 per cent of respondents confirmed proactive engagement on the Ukraine issue by schools. Activities included non-uniform days, appeals for charitable donations and paid-for advertisements in school newsletters … By way of contrast, there was widespread repression of Palestine solidarity seen in schools [that] made every effort to silence discussion of the Israeli attack on Palestine or educate children on the context and history of the region' (*Middle East Monitor*, 2022). As Yahya's mother said of her son's school, 'They were all for showing support for Ukraine. It's a double standard, and we will not accept it' (Kimber, 2023). The CAGE survey suggested that the disparity was 'a product of British government policies to manage and constrain the ability and opportunities to engage [in] topics such as these within schools' (CAGE International, 2022). Chapter 1 discusses why grief for innocent lives seems to have a geographical, political and racial hierarchy.

In 'Misrepresentation: a qualitative study on discourses on Islam, British values and identity affecting British Muslim pupils in Bradford and East London', a paper that I co-wrote with Dr Nasima Hassan, we interviewed students about their narratives (Coles & Hassan, 2017). On the next page is a response from a Muslim student from East London, who explained how her school used its authority to silence her counter-narrative while simultaneously promoting a more mainstream one.

CRITICAL PEDAGOGY: A TEACHER'S COMPANION

> 'Even in creative writing, I was told writing about drone attacks [in Syria] was too political and that I need to write something about my life instead. About my life? Are you joking me? But, I notice when we do anything good, like we raised money for Cancer Research, my friend Saba, she's from Syria too, she is always in the picture then up on the school website and in the paper. Then, the school tells us, I mean I read about it on the website, that they are concerned about Saba's family and care for the Syrians who have lost their families. I am so confused, man' – Jannah, Syrian, 15

A desire among students and teachers to explore different opinions and counter-narratives is not a reluctance to learn about mainstream and dominant narratives. Students 'are not choosing to remove themselves from the mainstream democratic system' (Ahmed, 2009). Instead, they want to be more aware of their world and, where possible, change it for the better. In Jannah's case, teachers and leaders in her school used their authority and power to prevent her from writing and learning about what was important to her – the first-hand experiences of her extended family in Syria. Yet the school was very keen to show the outside world, via its website and newspaper articles, that its students were socially conscious, charitable and had a stake in their society. Teachers, therefore, need to catalyse their students to 'fight against the corridors of power and enforce equality for themselves and others' (Coles, 2014a). Critical pedagogy is an integral tool that allows students – via their teachers – to understand how the structural and ideological mechanisms of schools operate. These mechanisms, if not interrogated and dismantled, will always promote the mainstream narrative.

CRITICAL RACE THEORY

Although this book does not look at critical race theory in extended detail, I encourage the reader to take time to investigate this further. Critical race theory is described as an approach that offers a 'lens through which to make sense of, deconstruct and challenge racial inequality in society' (Rollock & Gillborn, 2011). It explores the relationships between race, racism and power, and attempts to expose the racial inequality in society that operates through structures and assumptions. Critical race theory began as a legal movement in the mid 1970s after the advances of the civil rights era in the US in the 1960s. Using the theoretical writings of Derrick Bell, who is often credited with laying the foundation for critical race theory, it has more recently been implemented in the field of education. In relation to narratives, Daniel Solórzano and Tara Yosso suggest that naming racism, racial inequalities and racial oppression is necessary for racialised people to 'find their voice' (Solórzano & Yosso, 2002). Marginalised students must engage in 'hearing their own stories and the stories of others, listening to how the arguments against them are framed, and learning to make the arguments to defend themselves' (Solórzano & Yosso, 2002). Richard Delgado and Jean Stefancic, writing about narratives, encourage the important idea of the 'empathetic fallacy', where 'one can change a narrative by merely offering another' (Delgado & Stefancic, 2012). However, this is in the hope that empathy will quickly take over. Teachers must work relentlessly to challenge dominant narratives (including their own) by listening to, valuing and advocating the voices of their students.

ROLE MODELS

Lee Elliot Major of the University of Exeter is Britain's first professor of social mobility. He suggests that 'teachers may act differently towards children from working-class backgrounds' (Weale, 2023). His book *Equity in Education: levelling the playing field of learning*, co-written with Emily Briant, states: 'Most teachers come from middle-class backgrounds, yet they receive little or no preparation in how they might understand and engage with pupils and parents who come from different backgrounds' (Major & Briant, 2023). Major 'blames a mindset in education that treats working-class children as "inferior" and requires them to become "middle-class clones" in order to succeed in school' (Weale, 2023). 'We've been stuck in a deficit mindset for decades, trying to get children from working-class homes to fit into our middle-class system, rather than adapting the system itself to be less alienating,' Major and Briant write. Their book advocates for lessons to celebrate working-class achievement and feature important figures such as Tracey Emin, Mary Anning, Michael Faraday and Stormzy.

A recently published paper by researchers at Durham University found that there were 'proportionately more White British teachers than in the student intakes to schools' (Gorard et al., 2023). The paper highlights that 'due to the exceptional number of ethnic minority students, the disproportion (or mismatch) is worse in London than anywhere else'. The North East of England was found to have the 'least diverse teaching workforce in the country, with students of Pakistani or black-African origin likely to never have a teacher of similar ethnicity in their classrooms' (Ofori, 2023). The paper concludes that 'a student lacking any teachers of the same ethnic group might be treated differently at school, and there is some evidence that this might affect their attainment outcomes' (Gorard et al., 2023). Other research indicates that 'racially matched teacher role models have positive educational benefits for students of color in particular' (Goldhaber et al., 2019).

When we consider the educational experience of Muslim students, the government's Social Mobility Commission states that young Muslims 'already encounter significant barriers in the education system itself' (Stevenson et al., 2017). This is because 'teachers have either stereotypical or overly low expectations of young Muslims' and because there are 'insufficient Muslim teachers or other role models in schools'. James A. Banks suggests that if students of colour predominantly encounter white people in powerful positions in schools, they will struggle in 'developing democratic racial attitudes' (Banks, 2014). Writing about her own early years in education in the US, bell hooks powerfully describes how her Black female teachers at elementary school were 'on a mission' to 'ensure that we would fulfill our intellectual destiny' (hooks, 1994). Her teachers were determined to authentically get to know their students: 'They knew our parents, our economic status, where we worshipped, what our homes were like, and how we were treated in the family.' Teacher understanding of their students' identity is essential for academic success and for young people to seek self-emancipation.

Although many teachers may not share religious, cultural or class identities with their students, they should seek to understand, respect and value their students' multiple identities. Teachers who are role models will influence their students' 'confidence, self-esteem, aspiration and educational and post-educational attainment' (Stevenson et al., 2017).

However, effective role models don't necessarily need to be from similar backgrounds to their students. The only requirement for an effective role model is authenticity – an authentic ally can recognise, embrace and celebrate the multiple identities of their students.

To make this happen, teachers must value dialogic learning (involving ongoing talk between teacher and students). This is an essential aspect of critical pedagogy. However, before engaging in open discussions with young people, teachers must be self-reflexive, examining their own feelings, reactions and motives, and how these influence what they do or think in a particular situation. Educators must begin this journey of introspection by reflecting on the nature and functions of racism (this will be aided by engaging with critical race theory). The classroom teacher must 'get over any hesitation about race and racism so that they develop the confidence and capacity to engage in discussions with young people' (Arshad, 2012). Creating opportunities for dialogue about identity, between the learner and the teacher, will allow either 'sudden events or slow and gradual evolutions' (Husband et al., 2016) in any predetermined labelling of certain students by teachers. I have witnessed the transformative impact of encouraging my Muslim students to share their identities and narratives with their non-Muslim teacher (as described in chapter 1). When the tables are turned and shifts of power take place, there is greater potential for emancipatory acts (Coles & Hassan, 2017).

hooks discusses her own experience with white educators, describing the 'rare white teacher who dared to resist, who would not allow racist biases to determine how we were taught', and how this communicated the 'belief that learning at its most powerful could indeed liberate' (hooks, 1994). As well as being liberating and emancipating, dialogues in the classroom celebrate student narratives, providing a 'contrast between teachers' predictable and often oppressive stereotyping of … students and the rich varied reality of their lives in school, at home and on the streets with their peers' (Gillborn, 2008). Thus, labels (either predetermined by the teacher or enforced by media and political rhetoric) can be actively dismantled, and authentic narratives and identities can be celebrated in school contexts.

As described in the introduction, I have worked in a range of diverse schools and I therefore have experience of the complexities and differences in student demographics. The schools that I have chosen to work in predominantly serve Muslim students, mainly of a working-class South Asian heritage. As a white, non-Muslim educator, I know the importance of creating authentic opportunities for Muslim students to be comfortable in sharing their multiple identities, narratives and attachments with members of staff who are not like them. To begin tackling social injustices, we can engage with young people about the 'ways in which individual and collective identities matter to their everyday lives as young Britons' (Habib, 2017). Being open-minded and eager to find out about their students will allow teachers to respect and embrace their narratives, and to understand how *every* student can thrive and soar, not just the ones who look like them.

AGENCY

Democracy is not broken. Democracy has not ceased to be. Democracy is manipulated to allow some voices to be heard but not others. Once democracy has been nullified, so has the potential for action and agency. As James Baldwin suggests, the goal of democracy should be for everyone to improve their lives and raise themselves to a desirable level of happiness, security and possibility (Baldwin & Mead, 1971). This opportunity is not afforded to many people (owing to their class, ethnicity or religion, for example), so individual and collective agency is necessary to remedy this inequality. Schools and education are crucial for change to occur, because 'learning assumes a political dynamic as it becomes not only the condition for the acquisition of agency but also the sphere for imagining oppositional social change' (Giroux, 2004). Agency will come from political literacy, civic courage, historical awareness and a desire for the improvement of oneself and others. Without being exposed to different counter-narratives, we have no agency and therefore no reason for change.

Emancipatory education, through critical pedagogy, will inspire young people in a democratic society to appropriately and articulately criticise embedded mechanisms, practices and assumptions that are oppressive and harmful. Schooling should catalyse an informed distrust of what students read in the mainstream media, especially regarding misrepresentation and the promotion of dominant narratives. Teachers must work with young people to 'challenge the accepted social truths purveyed by media and education' (Coles, 2014b), in order for students to be 'able to critically analyze what is happening in the world and organize themselves to change it' (Kundnani, 2014). Critical pedagogues strive to collaborate with students to think critically about politics, history and representation through the power of counter-narratives. Schools must promote a pedagogy of freedom that allows young people to express their lived realities in safe spaces without fear of retribution or criminalisation (Habib, 2017). By using critical pedagogy in classrooms to promote authentic narratives, we can generate a true democracy that will initiate agency and social justice.

If teachers encourage authentic student narratives through critical pedagogy, students' personal experiences are promoted as essential teaching and learning resources that enable them to connect their own narratives, social relations and histories to what they study in school. Experience becomes the spark of enquiry and piques curiosity about how to overcome personal and collective struggles. A key principle of critical race theory is allowing the 'minority voice' to be heard and listened to. Teachers need only listen to their students to understand young people's beliefs, passions and concerns. A key idea is of a 'call to context' (Delgado & Stefancic, 2000), which challenges traditional and hegemonic ideas and 'emphasises the importance of experiential knowledge; paying attention and highlighting the voices and experiences of students of colour' (Coles & Hassan, 2017).

Another essential facet of critical race theory is storytelling (Delgado & Stefancic, 2000), specifically counter-storytelling – a form of narrative based on experience. Counter-storytelling can dismantle any embedded preconceptions held by teachers that may marginalise certain students. It can also help those students to discover, through sharing their stories, that other members of their class or school have had similar experiences. By paying attention to and valuing the voices and experiences of our students, we can begin to use their narratives for transformative education. White privilege can be interrogated by educators who encourage their students to have 'an educated mistrust of everything that has been indoctrinated before' (Coles, 2014b). Students can then start to appreciate the power of their own narratives in challenging racism and inspiring social change: 'Stories can name a type of discrimination; once named, it can be combated' (Delgado & Stefancic, 2000). There is, more than ever, a fundamental need for schools to promote authentic social justice to enhance the social consciousness, civic courage and agency of all young people, but most notably our marginalised and under-resourced students. To do this, teachers must recognise the importance of learning about their students' identities and understanding their lived experiences. As Stuart Hall insists, 'people have to invest something of themselves, something that they recognise is of them or speaks to their condition' (Hall & Back, 2011).

A PEDAGOGY OF IDENTITY

Critical pedagogy connects classroom learning with the experiences, histories and resources that every student brings with them to school. This can be referred to as a 'pedagogy of identity' – a pedagogy that holds the identity of the individual at the heart of education. A pedagogy of identity relies on narratives; educators must highlight authentic storytelling of identity and never underestimate its significance. Kristen Case suggests that schools should be places where teachers and students share 'moments of classroom grace' (Case, 2014) to interrogate their world and begin to question (however difficult) students' sense of agency. As Henry A. Giroux writes, 'education is always a moral and political practice that not only produces knowledge but also legitimates particular identities, modes of identification, desires, and narratives that support particular individual and social relations', and allows students to 'begin to question, however troubling, their sense of agency, relationships to others, and their relationship to the larger world' (Giroux, 2018). Developing a critical consciousness of the world will help young people to challenge injustices and promote social change. Critical pedagogy is, therefore, a continuous moral and political project that enables students to build a social awareness of freedom through a pedagogy of identity.

Traditional authoritarian structures need to be challenged and removed in schooling to allow the emancipatory acts of student narratives to be heard and celebrated. All students need to be free to speak about themselves, their lives and their hopes. Educators can encourage authentic and genuine viewpoints among the students in their schools, and actively listen to these narratives and respond in ways that help young people to learn about their world. Only when teachers encourage their students' narratives will authentic social justice happen.

This chapter opened with an example of how marginalised and oppressed voices are frequently criticised and silenced. Like Stormzy, the Black musician and poet Gil Scott-Heron is an important figure to critical pedagogues. His poem and song *The Revolution Will Not Be Televised* (1970) denounces the dominant white culture spread by the media. Scott-Heron describes how American capitalism is deliberately structured to prevent radical or revolutionary thought among the oppressed. Civic courage is replaced by possessions; the fight for equality is diluted by apathy and consumerism; consumers become stagnant spectators rather than architects of agency and action. Scott-Heron's lyrics urged audiences to protest and revolt. He reminded listeners that apathy must be contested, encouraging Black citizens to educate themselves about media indoctrination and rise up against oppression. This awakening is what we need for all our students.

SUGGESTIONS

Think about the curriculum that your school offers – the 'hidden' curriculum as well as the prescribed curriculum. Teachers should research the 'Why Is My Curriculum White?' campaign,[23] set up by University College London in 2014 to challenge the lack of diversity in education. As Mariya Hussain writes, Black and minority ethnic students 'find themselves unrepresented, their histories and cultures completely ignored in the academic field because for many years white writing and history has been given a higher standing' (Hussain, 2015). History should be the study of the disenfranchised, the oppressed and the people. All students should be given the space to identify with the history of their country and their cultures. If history is whitewashed then it may be regarded by many young people as an authoritative and definitive judgement of their insignificance, which could in turn foster alienation and even resentment.

---

23 www.dtmh.ucl.ac.uk/videos/curriculum-white

Think about the charitable endeavours that take place in your school. Are they chosen at random? Do members of staff usually select them? Is there a geographical or community link to the charities selected? Of course, it's important to support a variety of charities, but they must be carefully chosen. Using your students' experiences and narratives to inform these choices will have a powerful impact on their sense of belonging and inclusion.

Integral to critical pedagogy (and critical race theory) is encouraging narratives from your students. Listen to these narratives and learn something. A 'call to context' (Delgado & Stefancic, 2000) can act as a powerful tool to counter dangerous misinterpretation in the mainstream media. By creating a climate where student narratives can be explored, we work towards a number of goals. First, the dominant mainstream narrative is questioned and contested. Highlighting how power structures work will inspire students to be aware of their world and their part in it. Second, by encouraging students' counter-narratives, they learn that their opinions, fears and aspirations are respected and valued, and educators can begin to understand their students. Traditional hierarchical structures of authority are dismantled; teachers become learners and learners become teachers. Third, when counter-narratives are heard, authentic democracy and agency are promoted. We do not encourage counter-narratives and counter-storytelling in order to tick multicultural and inclusivity boxes, but to inspire action and change. Narratives can name and call out discrimination, racism and oppression. Only once these have been identified can they be combated.

Educators should create safe spaces where students can collaboratively explore how society works. Through education we can provide opportunities for young people to safely discuss and challenge. Creating the space and time to reflect upon counter-narratives can be powerful in helping young people to respond to the contradictions and conflicts they observe in the social world. A safe space is not the same as allowing freedom of speech, particularly as 'freedom' is often only bestowed on certain groups of people, usually white, secular and middle-class. Only certain people are allowed to speak freely, and only certain subjects are allowed to be freely discussed – the ones that are not perceived to be a critique of established norms. We need to create a culture where every student has the right to voice their educated opinion and share their narratives about lived realities without fear of incrimination or judgement.

With narratives comes transformational knowledge. Critical pedagogues must appreciate that education is always political as it always involves relations of power. I have been involved in organising events in schools to promote counter-narratives. These have included Q&A sessions where influential members of the local community (vicar, imam, journalist, police officer and school governor, for example) were invited to respond to student questions. One project that I organised for Year 9 students, called 'Your Voice', allowed all students the opportunity to work alongside local poets to write, practise and deliver spoken word performances on subjects that were important to them. Staff initially had reservations about this project – many were uncomfortable with the freedom their students were afforded. However, the results spoke for themselves. It was truly inspiring to watch students passionately and eloquently express themselves on subjects such as the misrepresentation of young people in the mainstream media, the 'invisible' social issue of homelessness, and the Israel-Palestine conflict. I think about those performances to this day, and I am confident that the students involved with 'Your Voice' do as well. As teachers, we need to be brave in supporting young people to speak openly and passionately, and to discuss their confusions and frustrations. In this way, students are likely to become confidently articulate, historically aware and politically literate – essential tools for self-emancipation.

CHAPTER 4
EMANCIPATION

In the preface, we began to discuss the true purpose of education. In 1787, the philosopher and social reformer Jeremy Bentham, 'writing when mechanistic technology and mass production were seen as key to the economic security and collective wellbeing of society' (Hopp, 2022), set out three aims for his pedagogical model of education: saving time, saving money and increasing academic aptitude. Sarah Hopp argues that the Benthamite system was based on 'control, enforcing prescribed and uniform thinking, and focusing on employability skills' (Hopp, 2022). In 2015, Nick Gibb delivered a speech on the purpose of education, stating that 'education is the engine of our economy' (Gibb, 2015b). Gibb's mission as schools minister was to create an education system with the central goal of promoting economic growth and global competitiveness. Here, it seems that the purpose of education is solely for financial profitability.

This aspiration continues with new research from Frontier Economics, commissioned by Ambition Institute 'to explore the economic benefits of high quality teaching' and show that 'great teaching is a key driver of economic growth' (Ambition Institute, 2023). The UK-based Ambition Institute provides 'evidence-based professional development programmes to train teachers and leaders' (Frontier Economics, 2023), such as National Professional Qualifications and Early Career Teacher induction, and is a 'largely government-funded teacher training charity' (Dickens, 2022).

The research suggests that 'the percentage increase in lifetime earnings for students exposed to five or more years of higher teaching quality ranges from 3% to 3.7%' and that the 'cumulative expected increase in lifetime earnings over the entire lifetime of pupils going through the school system in the next decade could reach up to £90bn' (Frontier Economics, 2023).

On initial reading, this may seem a positive forecast. However, when we look closely at other research, it appears that no matter how young people are taught and how well they achieve academically, socioeconomic status (which is often linked to class) and religion may remain barriers. In 2014, Nabil Khattab and Ron Johnston, using data from the Office for National Statistics Labour Force Survey of more than half a million people, found that 'Muslims are facing the worst job discrimination of any minority group in Britain' and 'had the lowest chance of being in work or in a managerial role' (Dobson, 2014). The government has acknowledged that 'Muslim job-seekers in the UK are disadvantaged ... facing significant pay gaps compared with those who identify as Christian' (*The Economic Times*, 2017). *The Independent* reported in 2014 that Muslim men are 'up to 76 per cent less likely to have a job of any kind compared to white, male British Christians of the same age and with the same qualifications. And Muslim women were up to 65 per cent less likely to be employed than white Christian counterparts' (Dobson, 2014).

More recent research indicates 'clear links between deprivation and achievement of first or upper second-class degrees and progression to highly skilled employment or higher study. Students from areas with higher deprivation levels have poorer outcomes than those from areas with low deprivation' (Bolton & Lewis, 2023). Despite attention-grabbing headlines such as 'Improving teaching could boost the UK economy by almost £10 billion' (Ambition Institute, 2023), it appears that our most disadvantaged or 'under-resourced' students (Major & Briant, 2023) may always experience inequality and discrimination in employment. The onus seems to be on individuals to attempt to improve themselves[24] through academic success, while structural inequalities of class, poverty and religion are systematically ignored.

---

24 A facet of neoliberalism explored further in this chapter.

If we believe that the purpose of education is ultimately to boost the economy, students from marginalised communities will only be educated to become employable, leaving 'no place for critical, creative and divergent thinking' (Hopp, 2022). But students in schools must be taught to think. As Martin Luther King, Jr explained, the 'function of education ... is to teach one to think intensively and to think critically' (King, 1992). But what should students actually think about? And, more importantly, what are secondary school students being told to think about?

E.D. Hirsch, Jr advocates for a school curriculum based on a common core of knowledge, in order to ensure that students become culturally literate (Hirsch, 1987). A 2010 paper by Fenwick English states that Hirsch's suggestion is that 'freezing a culture' (English, 2010) is necessary to allow essential content to become standardised. In other words, for knowledge to be unified and definitive, Hirsch believes it would be easier to look at a snapshot of time and ignore the fact that knowledge of the world is continually evolving and adapting. Bob Peterson, a fifth-grade teacher in the US, writes: 'After reading eight books by Hirsch it is clear that his view of "American literate culture" is overwhelming European-American based. Moreover, while Hirsch talks about the "classless character of cultural literacy" he virtually ignores the history, tradition, and literature of and about the working class and other marginalized groups and their conflicts with dominant society' (Peterson, 1994).

Insisting on an enforced and static historical cultural literacy means that secondary schools teach only certain theories, histories and ideas. As Henry A. Giroux suggests, this prevents any opportunity for teachers to 'make knowledge critical and transformative' (Giroux, 2016). When culture is frozen, so are the privileged and dominant social structures that define this cultural literacy. With echoes of Pierre Bourdieu, English argues that if schools adhere to the purpose of education advocated by Hirsch and supported by policymakers such as Gibb and the former UK education secretary Michael Gove, they will legitimise this cultural literacy and preserve the culture of the elites who are at the helm of social power. If schools teach a frozen culture, students will have the opportunity only to investigate a stagnant moment in time. A freezeframe of history tells our students (particularly our most marginalised, disadvantaged and under-resourced) that nothing can change.

If we want the world to be different (bearing in mind that some people, mainly those in control and power, do not want this, as it will change current hierarchies and power structures), we must teach students differently. Paulo Freire proposed that cultural literacy should in fact be an approach that encourages students to have a 'critical reading of reality' (Freire, 1983). This form of teaching is ultimately a political act. If we are to change society and combat inequalities and oppression, young people must first recognise these structures and causes, so that they, through agency and action, 'can create a new situation, one which makes possible the pursuit of a fuller humanity' (Freire, 1996). The written word is a tool that can be used to explore and critically analyse the world; critical pedagogy enables students to have a reading of the world using words. Reading the world means to understand how social, political and economic systems influence and manipulate history, language and culture to accentuate privilege for some and take away the opportunities of many. Therefore, the acts of reading the word (through knowledge) and reading the world (through awareness) can guide students to challenge existing structures of inequality and oppression. Critical pedagogy allows students to understand their world and, importantly, transform it for the better.

A PEDAGOGY OF EMANCIPATION

In this final chapter, we will look at how critical pedagogy can lead to emancipation - a pedagogy of emancipation, if you will. Emancipation is an act of liberation and freedom that can be collectively organised by teachers and students who seek social justice leading to social change. If teaching and learning enable the fostering of attitudes and dispositions advocated by critical pedagogy, this will lead to 'social justice, equality and empowerment' (McLaren, 2009). A pedagogy of emancipation involves placing great emphasis on teaching and learning that boldly foster critical reflection and consciousness, which will ultimately result in a socially just and fairer society.

Opportunities for liberatory discourses can be achieved if students and teachers engage in the learning of emancipatory knowledge. For this to happen, young people must be able to interrogate how 'social relationships are distorted and manipulated by relations of power and privilege' (McLaren, 2009). As discussed in chapter 3, students can offer counter-narratives to challenge the myths and barriers perpetuated by the powerful and the privileged in society. One of the goals of emancipatory education, through critical pedagogy, is 'liberation and freedom from controlling powers and conventions' (Coles, 2015) working towards a 'collective dedication to truth' (hooks, 1994). Emancipatory education draws on the tools of critical pedagogy in order to help young people 'contest the stories fabricated for them by "outsiders" and to construct counterstories that give shape and direction to the practice of hope and the struggle for an emancipatory politics of everyday life' (McLaren, 1995). Emancipatory knowledge guides students and their teachers to understand how institutions and structures operate. This type of learning is not about only memorising facts, dates and statistics. Although learning factual content is essential for educational achievement in various school subjects, education must also help young people to develop as reflective and active citizens who are determined to tackle social inequalities and injustices.

COLLECTIVE EMANCIPATION

Emancipatory education must not be solely about the individual, but also about the collective – about wider society. Freedom has always been about the work of groups, not individuals. According to Giroux, 'collective freedom provides the basic conditions for people to narrate their own lives, hold power accountable, and embrace a capacious notion of human dignity' (Giroux, 2013). Critical pedagogy, in its purest sense, will always attempt to combat forms of neoliberalism. Neoliberalism refers to a neoconservative social philosophy and economic theory that attempts to minimise state influence in the economy through privatisation and austerity (seen significantly during the Thatcher government of the 1980s). One tenet of neoliberalism is the encouragement of consumerism. Through individual consumption, material wealth is maximised, and this is presented as integral to our wellbeing and happiness. 'Decades of neoliberal policies have reshaped our world – but perhaps their deepest impact has been to corrode the bonds which underpinned society: replacing the collective with the individual' (Blakeley, 2021).

In education, also, it seems that the individual is far more important than the collective. Students are praised and rewarded for their individual success through grades and outcomes; the success of education as a whole is measured by personal achievement rather than collective improvement. This neoliberal education ensures that the individual is an 'isolated particle, floating freely in space – occasionally bumping up against other particles but really never becoming embedded in a community' (Blakeley, 2021). One of the goals of critical pedagogy is the improvement of the collective, because there can be no individual emancipation without wider societal transformation. Therefore, students need to understand themselves as individuals, as well as their role of being responsible for one another.

ENCULTURATION AND INTEREST CONVERGENCE

For many, the purpose of education is purely to 'better' the individual. Success is measured as the individual moving away – often upwardly – from their collective or community. So let's ask the question: is there anything wrong with our most disadvantaged and under-resourced students successfully passing tests and achieving good grades? Numerous 'successful' schools promote (through their websites and social media) their high-achieving Muslim or Black students who outperform other non-Muslim and non-Black students. But who is ultimately being represented as successful here – the students themselves or their school leaders? Many schools that teach marginalised students subject young people to a form of 'enculturation' (Osberg & Biesta, 2008) as a trade-off for academic success. Enculturation is the process by which students are taught to demonstrate and embody the values and behaviours deemed necessary to succeed, ultimately to ensure that the school is seen as successful. Curricula that promote only certain histories, authors and points of view encourage students to cast off their own 'inferior' backgrounds, values and cultures. Many students are led to believe that in order to succeed in education, they must absorb and accept 'superior' values, cultures and knowledge, assimilating into the (mainly white, middle-class and Eurocentric) school ethos. For example, learning the 'correct' knowledge from a whitewashed curriculum will help students from a minority background to succeed in examinations. In essence, the

English secondary education system is assessing not who the students are, but how white and middle class they can pretend to be.

Expecting students to perform well academically at the expense of their own identities is a perfect example of Derrick Bell's idea of 'interest convergence' (Bell, 1980). Interest convergence is an important element of critical race theory and is described as when the 'majority group tolerates advances for racial justice only when it suits its interest to do so' (Delgado & Stefancic, 2012). In other words, white people will support the success of non-white people only when there are benefits for them. In schools, academic advances by, for example, Black and Muslim students are encouraged and supported only when there are benefits to their (mainly white) schools and school leaders. White people may have very little incentive to work towards challenging, fighting and eradicating inequality, as this may cause a shift in the status quo, weakening their dominance and superiority. The academic success of our marginalised and under-resourced students is merely a vehicle for the career advancement and self-interest of school leaders.

Rather than prescribing a didactic and authoritarian teaching style focused on the neoliberal aspiration of individual success, critical pedagogy does something else. It enables young people and their teachers to work together in the classroom to pursue worthwhile collective goals of social justice as well as academic success. It is crucial for teachers and students to cooperate in classroom spaces when practising pedagogies of emancipation. Critical pedagogy subverts hierarchies and elitism to empower teachers and students to collaborate, so that they 'work together to create a schooling space that emboldens students' voices, stimulates dialogue and recommends reflection and action to attain goals' (Habib, 2017). Emancipatory knowledge searches out ways to fight inequality by encouraging spaces for collective agency and action.

SELF-EMANCIPATION

Authentic emancipation must be self-regulated, 'where the individual achieves emancipation rather than it being done to them' (Coles, 2015). Gert Biesta has criticised the model of critical pedagogy for emancipatory purposes, arguing that it 'does not foster student freedom but instead leads to new forms of dependency' (Moilanen & Huttunen, 2021). However, this problem can be overcome 'when emancipation is understood not as acquiring objective knowledge but as summoning students to independent thinking' (Moilanen & Huttunen, 2021). The critical pedagogue works hard for this continuing altruistic endeavour. Emancipation should not be seen as a form of 'graduation ceremony (getting the diploma from teacher for passing the exam)' (Draper, 1971), but rather as a process of struggle for young people who are seen by many, especially those in power, as unready (and, indeed, undeserving) of emancipation. Students will 'become ready for emancipation only by launching the struggle themselves, before anyone considers them ready for it' (Draper, 1971). To paraphrase Karl Marx, the emancipation of our students must be conquered by the students themselves. We must catalyse our students' fight for self-emancipation and constantly remind them that 'there is one, and only one, remedy. Help yourselves. Determine that you will not endure this abominable state of things any longer; act up to your determination, and it will vanish' (Weston et al., 1953).

The path of self-emancipation is a long and arduous one, across a terrain of systemic obstacles, and although teachers cannot be with their students every step of the way, they can clear paths and help them to gain the knowledge, skills and qualities necessary for their unique journeys. Fighting oppression is not simple, nor straightforward. It is always a struggle. Freire explains that to 'surmount the situation of oppression, people must first critically recognize its causes, so that through transforming action they can create a new situation, one which makes possible the pursuit of a fuller humanity' (Freire, 1996). Sometimes, highlighting the injustices and inequalities of our society can seem insensitive or cruel, but sheltering students from their realities can be more harmful in the long term. As teachers, we need to 'illuminate that darkness' (Baldwin, 1962) by teaching our students the attributes of civic courage, political literacy, articulated resistance and social responsibility. Students must match these attributes with awareness, compassion and determination to change their world for the better.

Freire promoted a progressive pedagogy of possibility and liberation, arguing that the traditional banking method of education was robotic and restrictive. Emancipatory strategies seek to encourage civic courage and social responsibility among students. Through critical pedagogy, students come to know that learning is 'not something done by teachers to students for their own good but is something students codevelop for themselves, led by a critical and democratic teacher' (Shor, 1992). New transformational knowledge is created by students and teacher as a collective, precluding any form of 'interest convergence' (Bell, 1980). As Giroux asks, 'How do we address education as a political project in which learning is central to creating informed citizens and catalyzing social change?' (Giroux, 2023). Enabling problem-posing pedagogy and critical inquiry that are relevant and pertinent to students' identities, where students formulate questions and solutions, provides a new avenue for effective social justice exploration in the classroom. Furthermore, a co-construction of what is relevant and important knowledge elevates the belief that teachers, young people and citizens can engage in reflective action for social justice and social change. Pedagogies that mobilise student engagement, participation and critical consciousness open up spaces for the language of hope and possibility.

If there is to be successful collaboration and communication in the classroom, dichotomous power relations must be resolved. If students and teachers are to rethink and resolve power relations then 'education must begin with the solution of the teacher-student contradiction, by reconciling the poles of the contradiction so that both are simultaneously teachers and students' (Freire, 1996). Knowledge is not the sole domain of the teacher; knowledge belongs to all and is shared. Teachers require hope and resilience in order to decentre their role. Many teachers will feel anxiety about losing their knowledge, expertise and perceived authority. And it can be extremely difficult for white educators to deploy emancipatory education, especially elements of critical race theory. Therefore, it is pleasing that several teacher training institutions (including Glasgow, Newcastle and Leeds Beckett universities) and schools are providing teachers with comprehensive anti-racism education that they can use to inform their classroom teaching and learning.

DANGEROUS THINKING[25]

There is a desperate need for 'voices of dangerous and courageous thinking' (Coles, 2015) in a time when teachers feel frustrated and disempowered because of the 'stagnant educational landscape, which currently seems unshakable and rebukes anyone who attempts to disrupt or subvert it' (Coles, 2015). Emancipatory teaching and learning, as some teachers already know, is all about taking risks. Risk is essential to ensure that 'students are not to be seen as objects to be molded and disciplined, but as subjects of action and responsibility' (Biesta, 2013). For critical pedagogues, this element of risk is essential as it propels them on in their drive towards emancipatory education. Critical pedagogy means that teachers consciously embrace risk, and have the courage and conviction to ensure that their students have the spaces and tools to tackle injustices and inequalities. Rather than dictate to educate, the teacher's role is to guide, encourage and facilitate learning that is emancipatory and ultimately self-emancipatory. A classroom that promotes critical pedagogy will pay attention to students' sense of agency by valuing and listening to their narratives, encouraging all to become reflective individuals of action and responsibility.

However, as bell hooks writes, 'I have often felt that this type of learning process is very hard; it's painful and troubling' (hooks, 1994). Thus, a critical pedagogy of hope and emancipation must be agreed, organised and consciously practised by students and teachers through collective processes of reflection and dialogue. This requires patience and new ways of perceiving pedagogies. Unlearning prescriptive approaches to education can take time.

Only if teachers are brave and take risks will young people seize their opportunities to speak up against systemic oppression and embedded structures. As Freire writes, 'one of the tasks of the progressive educator, through a serious, correct political analysis, is to unveil the opportunities for hope, no matter what the obstacles may be' (Freire, 2006). Students and teachers will face obstacles in the battle for social justice. Students will fear reprisals for speaking out, fear talking back, and fear a lack of support from their teachers and school. Teachers will fear being seen as

25   Giroux, 2015.

a radical, missing out on promotions and losing their job security. When I was interviewed by Iesha Small for her book *The Unexpected Leader* (2019), our conversations delved into my previous writing, in particular blog posts that discussed Prevent: 'He feels the Prevent strategy, especially in its original form, disproportionately affects young people in the types of communities that his school serves' (Small, 2019). We discussed the 'potentially career ending negative professional consequences' of these blog posts, and the fact that it would be easier, 'as a white middle-class man who is personally unaffected by some of the issues', to 'maintain the status quo' (Small, 2019). As soon as teachers recognise and confront the obstacles that face them and their students, they can begin to remove them. Emancipation relies on the teacher first. Only then can students learn to self-emancipate.

Emancipatory teachers might draw upon poignant and powerful recollections from history to motivate young people to speak up and talk back. In her memoir, the political activist Assata Shakur, a member of the Black Liberation Army in the 1970s, recalls the physical violence as well as the symbolic violence of the racist slurs she encountered after she was arrested in 1973 on suspicion of murder. A police officer told Shakur that 'white people created empires because they were more civilized than the rest of the world. White people created ballet and opera and symphonies. "Did you ever hear of a nigger writing a symphony?" he asked' (Shakur, 1987). As white officers wielded their supremacy over her, Shakur stayed quiet for fear of physical violence. She was prevented from speaking her truth. In the end, she shared this traumatic experience in her memoir – this was her way of speaking up and talking back. Another Black writer, Teju Cole, describes 'Writing as writing. Writing as rioting. Writing as righting. On the best days, all three' (Cole, 2014). Shakur's advice to oppressed people should resonate with all teachers and students embracing critical pedagogy and critical race theory: 'Nobody is going to give you the education you need to overthrow them. Nobody is going to teach you your true history, teach you your true heroes, if they know that that knowledge will help set you free' (Shakur, 1987).

PEDAGOGY OF HOPE

Transformative learning is crucial for all students. It may be difficult to achieve, but with serious thought, appreciation and care, it can happen. However, hope is vital. Without hope, we are hopeless, but sometimes hope on its own is not enough. This is why a pedagogy of hope must be advocated, one that is collectively organised and consciously embodied by students and teachers alike. Hope is essential for possibility – the possibility of social change – but in education it is insufficient and ineffective to envisage hope as merely an abstract concept. 'Hope has to be informed, concrete, and actionable' (Pedro-Carañana & Giroux, 2017). As teachers, we need to create opportunities for our students to develop a 'hope in action – that is, a new force of collective resistance and a vehicle for anger transformed into collective struggle, a principle for making despair unconvincing and struggle possible' (Pedro-Carañana & Giroux, 2017). Resistance can be seen as an action and anger as an energy; both can be used by the critical pedagogue to collectivise and mobilise all their students with the goal of achieving authentic social justice. Both hope and possibility must be embraced in the classroom, alongside the need for critical reflection and consciousness.

A critical pedagogue must always have hope in their fight. It is important to consider that hope is a far more powerful attribute than optimism. Yes, a teacher must always be optimistic that they can expose, challenge and eradicate systemic inequality through education, but optimism suggests that this change will inevitably happen without any intervention. A form of educated hope is needed, allowing teachers and students to believe that emancipation can be successfully fought for through a collective approach and organised agency.

Without hope, any critique of power structures in the classroom can quickly descend into helplessness, inertia and apathy. A common critique of critical pedagogy (and especially critical race theory) is that it leads to pessimistic viewpoints and a sense of despair. Therefore, a collective, ongoing, positive moral agenda is needed from every teacher and every student to fight against social injustice and inequalities. Alongside hope, the critical pedagogue must keep a real sense of possibility within their fight. If we refuse to fight, or we refute that the fight actually exists, the future will be no more than a mirror image of the past and present.

> 'Hope, however, does not consist in crossing one's arms and waiting. As long as I fight, I am moved by hope; and if I fight with hope, then I can wait' – Freire, 1996

SUGGESTIONS

Critical Pedagogy: a teacher's companion has allowed the reader to understand what critical pedagogy is, and why there is an essential need for it in secondary schools in England. The chapters have explored four key themes of critical pedagogy: neutrality, teaching, narratives and, in this chapter, emancipation.

The book aims to catalyse an informed dialogue between committed educators, in the hope that they will act upon the recommendations and practices of critical pedagogy. However, it would be unrealistic if I were to expect that my arguments would be met by everyone with complete agreement. I am also conscious that this book will potentially be overlooked, disregarded and challenged without authority.[26] Despite these reservations, my hope is that *Critical Pedagogy: a teacher's companion* confronts predetermined assumptions, stimulates emotions, creates cognitive and moral challenges, and ultimately provokes dialogue.

Below is a list of what a critical pedagogue believes in, what they stand for and what they relentlessly strive for. These attributes, principles and values are what every teacher must inhabit to ensure that the moral, ethical and political undertaking of critical pedagogy has the opportunity to flourish and lead to authentic emancipation for all our students.

The teacher who advocates and embodies critical pedagogy:

1. Is always political and never neutral, as an apolitical neutral teacher seemingly sides against the students they have a duty of care for.

2. Constantly examines their own privilege, assumptions and beliefs, in order to make their students' histories, cultures and real lives central to the act of liberation and emancipation.

---

26   'Let them come right out with their defense of the indefensible' (Freire, 2006).

3. Recognises that knowledge is essential for understanding, but that this understanding must be used by their students alongside awareness, articulation, representation and agency.

4. Promotes the power of literacy, which enables their students to read their own world and to write their own history.

5. Remains clear that, without their students, their teaching is merely an act of delivery.

6. Knows the importance of authority in learning, but ensures that their authority does not lead to authoritative teaching.

7. Becomes a transformative intellectual who encourages democracy by allowing their students to be curious, to challenge societal authority and to critique inequalities.

8. Is always self-reflexive[27] in their evaluations, practices and teachings, in order to constantly strive and fight for what they believe is right.

9. Authentically listens, shares, values and embraces the voices and narratives of all their students.

10. Appreciates that self-emancipation is often a long, arduous and hazardous path, but one that they will work to illuminate on their students' unique journeys.

11. Understands that highlighting injustices and inequalities for their students may seem insensitive or cruel, but knows that sheltering students from their realities can be more harmful in the long term.

12. Does not settle for their students gaining a seat at the table; instead, their relentless goal is for all students to build their own table.

13. Focuses on collective action and agency above individual gratification and success.

14. Believes in dangerous and subversive thinking, taking risks and teaching against the grain.

15. Always has hope in their fight, as hope is a far more powerful tool than optimism.

16. Understands the importance of love.

---

27 Able to examine their own feelings, reactions and motives, and how these influence what they do or think in a situation.

'Love is an act of courage, not of fear, love is commitment to others. No matter where the oppressed are found, the act of love is commitment to their cause – the cause of liberation' – Freire, 1996

BIBLIOGRAPHY

Ahmed, S. (2009) *Seen and Not Heard: voices of young British Muslims*, Policy Research Centre

Ambition Institute. (2023) 'Improving teaching could boost the UK economy by almost £10 billion'. Retrieved from: www.ambition.org.uk/news/improving-teaching-could-boost-the-uk-economy-by-almost-10-billion   (accessed: 07/10/23)

Apple, M.W. (1993) 'The politics of official knowledge: does a national curriculum make sense?', *Teachers College Record*, 95(2), pp.222-241

Applebaum, A. (2015) 'How to regain control of Europe', *Slate*. Retrieved from: slate.com/news-and-politics/2015/11/the-paris-attacks-have-nothing-to-do-with-refugees-this-operation-was-planned-by-people-who-know-paris.html (accessed: 05/12/23)

Arshad, R. (2012) 'The twenty-first century teacher needs to engage with race and racism' in R. Arshad, T. Wrigley & L. Pratt (eds), *Social Justice Re-Examined: dilemmas and solutions for the classroom teacher* (pp.193-207), Trentham

Au, W. (2011) 'Teaching under the new Taylorism: high-stakes testing and the standardization of the 21st century curriculum', *Journal of Curriculum Studies*, 43(1), pp.25-45

Babiak, P. (2006) 'Manufactured cynicism: a review interview of *Against the New Authoritarianism*', *SubTerrain Magazine*, 5(44), pp.43-45. Retrieved from: www.humanities.mcmaster.ca/~girouxh/Manufactured_Cynicism.htm (accessed: 02/01/24)

Baldwin, J. (1962) 'The creative process' in *Creative America*, Ridge Press

Baldwin, J. & Mead, M. (1971) *A Rap on Race*, Lippincott

Banks, J.A. (2014) *An Introduction to Multicultural Education* (fifth edition), Pearson

Bell, D.A. (1980) 'Brown v. Board of Education and the interest-convergence dilemma', *Harvard Law Review*, 93(3), pp.518-533

Benn, H. (2015) 'Syria vote: read Hilary Benn's speech in full', *The Independent*. Retrieved from: www.independent.co.uk/news/uk/politics/syria-vote-read-hilary-benns-speech-in-full-a6758291.html (accessed: 05/11/23)

Benn, T. (1998) 'Don't Arab and Iraqi women weep when their children die?' Retrieved from: speakola.com/political/tony-benn-response-to-iraq-bombing-1998 (accessed: 05/11/23)

Bennett, T. (2017) 'Let's stop relying on hunches – it's time to use evidence to fix behaviour in schools', *The Guardian*. Retrieved from: www.theguardian.com/teacher-network/2017/nov/01/lets-stop-relying-on-hunches-its-time-to-use-evidence-to-fix-behaviour-in-schools (accessed: 02/01/24)

Bennett, T. (2018) 'Criticism pedagogy is an ideology based on Marxism. I'm ok with teaching children about Marxism. I'm ok with them becoming Marxists. I'm not ok with teaching them to be Marxists', X. Retrieved from: x.com/tombennett71/status/963157751026409474 (accessed: 12/12/23)

Bentham, J. (1787) *Panopticon; Or, the Inspection-House*, Payne

Bentley, L. (1999) 'A brief biography of Paulo Freire', *Pedagogy and Theatre of the Oppressed* (blog). Retrieved from: ptoweb.org/aboutpto/a-brief-biography-of-paulo-freire (accessed: 11/03/23)

Bernstein, B. (1971) *Class, Codes and Control: theoretical studies towards a sociology of language*, Routledge

Biesta, G.J.J. (2012) 'Giving teaching back to education: responding to the disappearance of the teacher', *Phenomenology & Practice*, 6(2), pp.35-49

Biesta, G.J.J. (2013) *The Beautiful Risk of Education*, Paradigm

Blakeley, G. (2021) 'How neoliberalism created a society of individuals', *Tribune*. Retrieved from: tribunemag.co.uk/2021/01/how-neoliberalism-created-a-society-of-individuals (accessed: 05/02/23)

Boakye, J. (2022) 'Why are books on the English school curriculum still in the grip of straight, white men?', *The Guardian*. Retrieved from: www.theguardian.com/commentisfree/2022/jun/07/books-english-curriculum-straight-white-men-children-need-broader-range (accessed: 20/05/23)

Bolton, P. & Lewis, J. (2023) *Equality of Access and Outcomes in Higher Education in England: research briefing*, House of Commons Library. Retrieved from: researchbriefings.files.parliament.uk/documents/CBP-9195/CBP-9195.pdf (accessed: 07/10/23)

Bourdieu, P. (1974) 'The school as a conservative force: scholastic and cultural inequalities' in J. Eggleston (ed), *Contemporary Research in the Sociology of Education* (pp.32-46), Methuen

CAGE International. (2022) 'CAGE briefing: understanding Ukraine and Palestine solidarity in UK schools'. Retrieved from: www.cage.ngo/articles/cage-briefing-understanding-ukraine-and-palestine-solidarity-in-uk-schools (accessed: 06/01/24)

Case, K. (2014) 'The other public humanities', *The Chronicle of Higher Education*. Retrieved from: www.chronicle.com/article/the-other-public-humanities (accessed: 06/01/24)

Chomsky, N. (1989) *Necessary Illusions: thought control in democratic societies*, South End Press

Christodoulou, D. (2014) 'Teaching knowledge is not indoctrination', *Daisy Christodoulou* (blog). Retrieved from: daisychristodoulou.com/2014/03/teaching-knowledge-is-not-indoctrination (accessed: 13/03/23)

Cole, T. (2014) 'Writing as writing. Writing as rioting. Writing as righting. On the best days, all three', X. Retrieved from: x.com/tejucole/status/454646310994710528 (accessed: 02/09/23)

Coles, T. (2014a) *Never Mind the Inspectors: here's punk learning*, Independent Thinking Press

Coles, T. (2014b) 'Critical pedagogy: schools must equip students to challenge the status quo', *The Guardian*. Retrieved from: www.theguardian.com/teacher-network/teacher-blog/2014/feb/25/critical-pedagogy-schools-students-challenge (accessed: 05/12/23)

Coles, T. (2015) 'Is the education system in this country f#%ked? Education, inequality and economic fodder' in I. Gilbert (ed), *There is Another Way: the second big book of independent thinking* (pp.131-138), Independent Thinking Press

Coles, T. & Hassan, N. (2017) 'Misrepresentation: a qualitative study on discourses on Islam, British values and identity affecting British Muslim pupils in Bradford and East London' in R. Race (ed), *Advancing Multicultural Dialogues in Education* (pp.53-69), Palgrave Macmillan

Colgan, J.D. (2013) 'Oil, conflict, and US national interests', *Quarterly Journal: International Security*. Retrieved from: www.belfercenter.org/publication/oil-conflict-and-us-national-interests (accessed: 20/05/23)

Collins, T. (2015) 'Hilary Benn's speech was the speech of a true leader', *The Telegraph*. Retrieved from: www.telegraph.co.uk/news/politics/labour/12031057/Hilary-Benns-speech-was-the-speech-of-a-true-leader.html (accessed: 05/12/23)

Culp, B. (2014) 'An analysis of future coaches' emerging dispositions on social justice: the wooden effect', *International Journal of Sports Science & Coaching*, 9(1), pp.111-122

Cushing, I. (2021) 'Language, discipline and "teaching like a champion"', *British Educational Research Journal*, 47(1), pp.23-41

De Beauvoir, S. (1955) 'La pensee de droite, aujourd'hui', *Privileges*, Gallimard

Delgado, R. & Stefancic, J. (2000) *Critical Race Theory: the cutting edge* (second edition), Temple University Press

Delgado, R. & Stefancic, J. (2012) *Critical Race Theory: an introduction* (third edition), New York University Press

Department for Education. (2014) *Promoting Fundamental British Values as Part of SMSC in Schools*. Retrieved from: www.gov.uk/government/publications/promoting-fundamental-british-values-through-smsc (accessed: 25/06/23)

Department for Education. (2016) *Eliminating Unnecessary Workload Around Planning and Teaching Resources: report of the Independent Teacher Workload Review Group*. Retrieved from: assets.publishing.service.gov.uk/government/uploads/system/uploads/attachment_data/file/511257/Eliminating-unnecessary-workload-around-planning-and-teaching-resources.pdf (accessed: 13/03/23)

Department for Education. (2021) 'Education secretary puts climate change at the heart of education'. Retrieved from: www.gov.uk/government/news/education-secretary-puts-climate-change-at-the-heart-of-education--2 (accessed: 20/05/23)

Department for Education. (2022a) 'Political impartiality guidance for schools – what you need to know' (blog post). Retrieved from: educationhub.blog.gov.uk/2022/02/17/political-impartiality-guidance-for-schools-what-you-need-to-know (accessed: 03/01/24)

Department for Education. (2022b) 'How Pupils Learn' exemplar materials. Retrieved from: https://assets.publishing.service.gov.uk/media/637b7702e90e0728475ed534/How_Pupils_Learn_Exemplars.pdf (accessed: 02/01/24)

Department for Education. (n.d.) *What You Need to Know About Political Impartiality in Schools*. Retrieved from: assets.publishing.service.gov.uk/media/61f137688fa8f5058a4b2f44/6.7731_DfE_Political_Impartiality_Guidance_Pamphlet_WEB__004_.pdf (accessed: 09/01/24)

Dewey, J. (1938) *Experience and Education*, Kappa Delta Pi

Díaz, K. (n.d.) 'Paulo Freire (1921-1997)', *Internet Encyclopedia of Philosophy*. Retrieved from: iep.utm.edu/freire (accessed: 11/03/23)

Dickens, J. (2022) 'DfE settles with Ambition over £121m Institute of Teaching contract dispute', *Schools Week*. Retrieved from: schoolsweek.co.uk/dfe-settles-with-ambition-over-121m-iot-contract-dispute (accessed: 07/10/23)

Dobson, R. (2014) 'British Muslims face worst job discrimination of any minority group, according to research', *The Independent*. Retrieved from: www.independent.co.uk/news/uk/home-news/british-muslims-face-worst-job-discrimination-of-any-minority-group-9893211.html (accessed: 05/12/23)

Draper, H. (1971) 'The principle of self-emancipation in Marx and Engels', *Socialist Register*, pp.81-109. Retrieved from: www.marxists.org/archive/draper/1971/xx/emancipation.html (accessed: 05/12/23)

English, F.W. (2010) 'The ten most wanted enemies of American public education's school leadership', *University Council for Educational Administration Review*, 51(3), pp.13-18

Eppley, K. & Dudley-Marling, C. (2019) 'Does direct instruction work? A critical assessment of direct instruction research and its theoretical perspective', *Journal of Curriculum and Pedagogy*, 16(1), pp.35-54

Fares, E. (2015) 'From Beirut, this is Paris: in a world that doesn't care about Arab lives', *HuffPost*. Retrieved from: www.huffingtonpost.com/elie-fares/beirut-paris-world-doesnt-care-arab-lives_b_8568140.html (accessed: 05/12/23)

Figueiredo, G.D.O., Siqueira, V.H.F.D. & Silva, A.C.D. (2021) 'Updating critical ideas in the 21st century to fight against the neoliberal machine: an interview with Professor Henry Giroux', *Praxis educativa*, 16

França, J. (2019) 'Henry Giroux: "Those arguing that education should be neutral are really arguing for a version of education in which nobody is accountable"', *CCCBLAB*. Retrieved from: lab.cccb.org/en/henry-giroux-those-arguing-that-education-should-be-neutral-are-really-arguing-for-a-version-of-education-in-which-nobody-is-accountable (accessed: 03/01/24)

Freire, P. (1983) 'The importance of the act of reading', *The Journal of Education*, 165(1), pp.5-11

Freire, P. (1985) *The Politics of Education: culture, power and liberation*, Bergin & Garvey

Freire, P. (1996) *Pedagogy of the Oppressed*, Penguin

Freire, P. (1998) *Pedagogy of Freedom: ethics, democracy and civic courage*, Rowman & Littlefield

Freire, P. (2006) *Pedagogy of Hope: reliving Pedagogy of the Oppressed*, Continuum

Frontier Economics. (2023) *The Economic Value of High Teaching Quality in the UK*. Retrieved from: s3.eu-west-2.amazonaws.com/ambition-institute/documents/The_economic_value_of_higher_teaching_quality_in_the_uk_1.pdf (accessed: 07/10/23)

Gannon, K. (2017) 'Paulo Freire, *Pedagogy of the Oppressed*, and a revolutionary praxis for education, part II', *Age of Revolutions*. Retrieved from: ageofrevolutions.com/2017/07/19/paulo-freire-pedagogy-of-the-oppressed-and-a-revolutionary-praxis-for-education-part-ii (accessed: 06/03/23)

Ghani, H. & Nagdee, I. (2018) *The Experience of Muslim Students in 2017-18*, NUS. Retrieved from: nusdigital.s3.eu-west-1.amazonaws.com/document/documents/41267/29d43267ae2f2f0906450a27487fcd36/The_Experience_of_Muslim_Students_in_2017-18.pdf (accessed: 07/12/23)

Gibb, N. (2015a) 'How E.D. Hirsch came to shape UK government policy' in J. Simons & N. Porter (eds), *Knowledge and the Curriculum: a collection of essays to accompany E. D. Hirsch's lecture at Policy Exchange*, Policy Exchange. Retrieved from: policyexchange.org.uk/wp-content/uploads/2016/09/knowledge-and-the-curriculum.pdf (accessed: 07/12/23)

Gibb, N. (2015b) 'The purpose of education', Department for Education. Retrieved from: www.gov.uk/government/speeches/the-purpose-of-education (accessed: 08/01/23)

Gibb, N. (2021) 'Nick Gibb: My advice to my successors at Education. Don't scrap GCSEs or ease up on standards', *ConservativeHome*. Retrieved from: conservativehome.com/2021/09/20/nick-gibb-my-advice-to-my-successors-at-education-dont-scrap-gcses-and-ease-up-on-standards (accessed: 15/12/23)

Gillborn, D. (2008) *Racism and Education: coincidence or conspiracy?*, Routledge

Giroux, H.A. (2004) 'Cultural studies, public pedagogy, and the responsibility of intellectuals', *Communication and Critical/Cultural Studies*, 1(1), pp.59-79

Giroux, H.A. (2010) 'Paulo Freire and the crisis of the political', *Power and Education*, 2(3), pp.335-340

Giroux, H.A. (2011) *On Critical Pedagogy*, Continuum

Giroux, H.A. (2013) 'Angela Davis, education and the meaning of freedom', *HuffPost*. Retrieved from: www.huffpost.com/entry/angela-davis_b_3055913 (accessed: 07/10/23)

Giroux, H.A. (2015) *Dangerous Thinking: in the age of the new authoritarianism*, Routledge

Giroux, H.A. (2016) 'Why teachers matter in dark times', *Truthout*. Retrieved from: truthout.org/articles/why-teachers-matter-in-dark-times (accessed: 06/12/23)

Giroux, H.A. (2018) 'Higher education and the politics of the radical imagination', *PRISM: Casting New Light on Learning, Theory and Practice*, 2(1), pp.23-43

Giroux, H.A. (2019) 'Toward a pedagogy of educated hope under casino capitalism', *Pedagogía y Saberes*, 50, pp.147-151

Giroux, H.A. (2023) 'Educators as public intellectuals in an age of tyranny: confront, fight back and organize', *CounterPunch*. Retrieved from: www.counterpunch.org/2023/09/26/educators-as-public-intellectuals-in-an-age-of-tyranny-confront-fight-back-and-organize (accessed: 30/09/23)

Goldhaber, D., Theobald, R. & Tien, C. (2019) 'Why we need a diverse teacher workforce', *Kappan*. Retrieved from: kappanonline.org/why-we-need-diverse-teacher-workforce-segregation-goldhaber-theobald-tien (accessed: 06/12/23)

Gorard, S., Chen, W., Tan, Y., See, B.H., Gazmuri, C., Tereshchenko, A., Demie, F. & Siddiqui, N. (2023) 'The disproportionality of ethnic minority teachers in England: trends, patterns, and problems', *Routledge Open Research*, 2, p.13

Gramsci, A. (1971) *Selections from the Prison Notebooks of Antonio Gramsci*, International Publishers

Gramsci, A. (2000) 'Men or machines?' in D. Forgacs (ed), *The Gramsci Reader: selected writings, 1916-1935*, NYU Press

Gruenewald, D.A. (2003) 'The best of both worlds: a critical pedagogy of place', *Educational Researcher*, 32(4), pp.3-12

Habib, S. (2017) *Learning and Teaching British Values: policies and perspectives on British identities*, Palgrave Macmillan

Hall, R. (2023) 'Books by female authors studied by just 2% of GCSE pupils, finds study', *The Guardian*. Retrieved from: www.theguardian.com/education/2023/mar/02/books-by-female-authors-studied-by-just-2-of-gcse-pupils-finds-study (accessed: 20/05/23)

Hall, S. & Back, L. (2011) 'At home and not at home' in C. Alexander (ed) *Stuart Hall and 'Race'* (pp.202-231), Routledge

Hall, S. (1996) 'Introduction: Who needs "identity"?' in S. Hall and P. Du Gay (eds), *Questions of Cultural Identity* (pp.1-17), Sage

Hirsch, Jr, E.D. (1987) *Cultural Literacy: what every American needs to know*, Houghton Mifflin

Hirsch, Jr, E.D. (1996) *The Schools We Need and Why We Don't Have Them*, Doubleday Books

hooks, b. (1993) 'bell hooks speaking about Paulo Freire – the man, his work' in P. Leonard & P. McLaren (eds), *Paulo Freire: a critical encounter*, Routledge

hooks, b. (1994) *Teaching to Transgress: education as the practice of freedom*, Routledge

Hopp, S. (2022) 'What is the purpose of education?', *The Optimus Blog*. Retrieved from: blog.optimus-education.com/what-purpose-education (accessed: 25/01/23)

Husband, C., Alam, Y., Huettermann, J. & Fomina, J. (2016) *Lived Diversities: space, place and identities in the multi-ethnic city*, Policy Press

Hussain, M. (2015) 'Why is my curriculum white?', NUS

Ireh, M. (2016) 'Scientific management still endures in education'. Retrieved from: files.eric.ed.gov/fulltext/ED566616.pdf (accessed: 22/01/24)

Jankowski, L. (2021) 'Biography of bell hooks, feminist and anti-racist theorist and writer', *ThoughtCo*. Retrieved from: www.thoughtco.com/bell-hooks-biography-3530371 (accessed: 18/03/23)

Kimber, C. (2023) 'Parents and students defend free speech on Palestine at east London school', *Socialist Worker*. Retrieved from: socialistworker.co.uk/palestine-2023/parents-and-students-defend-free-speech-on-palestine-at-east-london-school (accessed: 03/01/24)

King, Jr, M.L. (1992) 'The purpose of education' in C. Carson (ed), *The Papers of Martin Luther King, Jr. Volume I: called to serve, January 1929-June 1951* (pp.122-124), University of California Press

Krayem, G. (2018) 'As Muslim women we don't need you to speak for us, and we don't need to be saved', *The Guardian.* Retrieved from: www.theguardian.com/ commentisfree/2018/feb/23/as-muslim-women-we-dont-need-you-to-speak-for-us-and-we-dont-need-to-be-saved (accessed: 06/12/23)

Kundnani, A. (2014) *The Muslims are Coming! Islamophobia, extremism and the domestic war on terror,* Verso

Lais, H. (2017) 'As a history teacher, I'm horrified by the whitewashing of my curriculum – I'm being told to teach that colonialism was good', *The Independent.* Retrieved from: www.independent.co.uk/voices/black-history-month-colonialism-history-teacher-whitewashing-selective-past-a8025741. html (accessed: 20/05/23)

Lemov, D. (2010) *Teach Like a Champion: 49 Techniques that Put Students on the Path to College,* Jossey-Bass

Lemov, D. (2015) *Teach Like a Champion 2.0: 62 Techniques that Put Students on the Path to College,* Jossey-Bass

Lemov, D. (2021) *Teach Like a Champion 3.0: 63 Techniques that Put Students on the Path to College,* Jossey-Bass

Litner, B. (1990) *Exploring Critical Revision as a Process of Empowerment* (PhD dissertation), University of Toronto

Major, L.E. & Briant, E. (2023) *Equity in Education: levelling the playing field of learning,* John Catt

McIntosh, P. (1989) 'White privilege: unpacking the invisible knapsack', *Peace and Freedom Magazine,* pp.10-12. Retrieved from: admin.artsci. washington.edu/sites/adming/files/unpacking-invisible-knapsack.pdf (accessed: 08/01/24)

McKew, Q. (2020) 'US: We must elevate black voices to break down racial inequality' (blog post), Article 19. Retrieved from: www.article19.org/resources/ blog-by-quinn-mckew-we-must-elevate-black-voices-to-breakdown-racial-inequality (accessed: 22/01/24)

McLaren, P. (1995) *Critical Pedagogy and Predatory Culture: oppositional politics in a postmodern era,* Routledge

McLaren, P. (2009) 'Critical pedagogy: a look at the major concepts' in A. Darder, M.P. Baltodano & R.D. Torres (eds), *The Critical Pedagogy Reader* (second edition) (pp.61-83), Routledge

McNutt, C. (2021) 'Empty pedagogy, behaviorism, and the rejection of equity', *Medium*. Retrieved from: medium.com/human-restoration-project/empty-pedagogy-behaviorism-and-the-rejection-of-equity-c9d0fad15838 (accessed: 21/05/23)

Membis, L. (2011) 'Invisible women: Black Britons struggle to be heard', CNN. Retrieved from: edition.cnn.com/2011/10/14/world/europe/black-british-women/index.html (accessed: 07/12/23)

Middle East Monitor. (2022) 'Survey exposes UK government's "hypocrisy" over Ukraine and Palestine'. Retrieved from: www.middleeastmonitor. com/20220727-survey-exposes-uk-governments-hypocrisy-over-ukraine-and-palestine (accessed: 06/01/24)

Mirza, H.S. (2015) 'Decolonizing higher education: black feminism and the intersectionality of race and gender', *Journal of Feminist Scholarship*, 7, pp.1-13

Modood, T. (2013) *Multiculturalism*, Polity

Moilanen, A. & Huttunen, R. (2021) 'The German logic of emancipation and Biesta's criticism of emancipatory pedagogy', *Educational Theory*, 71(6), pp.717-741

Moreira da Silva, J. (2022) 'A tribute to bell hooks: for a revolution in education', *SOAS History Blog*. Retrieved from: blogs.soas.ac.uk/soashistoryblog/2022/03/08/a-tribute-to-bell-hooks-for-a-revolution-in-education (accessed: 18/03/23)

Morrison, N. (2020) 'Uncommon U-turn should help consign no excuses schools to history', *Forbes*. Retrieved from: www.forbes.com/sites/nickmorrison/2020/08/24/uncommon-u-turn-should-consign-no-excuses-culture-to-history (accessed: 27/05/23)

Nagdee, I., Ghani, H. & Ibrahim, Z. (eds) (2017) *Preventing Prevent: handbook 2017*, NUS Black Students. Retrieved from: www.preventwatch.org/wp-content/uploads/2021/08/Preventing_Prevent_Handbook_2017.pdf (accessed: 03/01/24)

NAHT. (2023) *Crisis Point: school leadership survey 2023*. Retrieved from: https://www.naht.org.uk/Portals/0/PDF's/Reports/Workload-and-wellbeing-report-Dec%202023-FINAL-UPDATED-2.pdf?ver=2023-12-14-162404-897 (accessed: 21/12/23)

Oborne, P. (2015) 'Paris attacks: we need calm and sense, not reactionism', *Middle East Eye*. Retrieved from: www.middleeasteye.net/columns/paris-attacks-we-need-calm-and-sense-not-reactionism-2032119349 (accessed: 07/12/23)

Ofori, M. (2023) 'Lack of diversity in teaching in England means minority ethnic pupils miss out', *The Guardian*. Retrieved from: www.theguardian.com/education/2023/aug/29/lack-diversity-teaching-means-minority-ethnic-pupils-england-miss-out (accessed: 02/09/23)

Open Society Foundations. (2016) *Eroding Trust: the UK's Prevent counter-extremism strategy in health and education*. Retrieved from: www.justiceinitiative.org/uploads/f87bd3ad-50fb-42d0-95a8-54ba85dce818/eroding-trust-20161017_0.pdf (accessed: 03/01/24)

Osberg, D. (2005) 'Redescribing "education" in complex terms', *Complicity: an international journal of complexity and education*, 2(1)

Osberg, D. & Biesta, G. (2008) 'The emergent curriculum: navigating a complex course between unguided learning and planned enculturation', *Journal of Curriculum Studies*, 40(3), pp.313-328

Osborne, S. (2017) 'US-led coalition air strike in Syria kills more than 30 people in school near Isis-held Raqqa, says human rights watchdog', *The Independent*. Retrieved from: www.independent.co.uk/news/world/middle-east/s-coalition-syria-air-strike-raqq-isis-school-killed-al-mansoura-human-rights-observatory-a7642781.html (accessed: 07/12/23)

Pedro-Carañana, J. & Giroux, H.A. (2017) 'Henry Giroux, public intellectual, on the menace of Trump and the new authoritarianism', *OpenDemocracy*. Retrieved from: www.opendemocracy.net/en/henry-giroux-public-intellectual-on-menace-of-trump-and-new-authori (accessed: 07/12/23)

Peterson, B. (1994) 'What should kids learn?', *Rethinking Schools*, 8(2). Retrieved from: rethinkingschools.org/articles/what-should-kids-learn (accessed: 22/01/24)

Platell, A. (2018) 'Can't you show a scintilla of gratitude, Stormzy?', *Daily Mail*. Retrieved from: www.dailymail.co.uk/debate/article-5429041/Platells-People-Stormzy-gratitude.html (accessed: 07/12/23)

Porter, N. & Simons, J. (2015) 'Foreword', *Knowledge and the Curriculum: a collection of essays to accompany E. D. Hirsch's lecture at Policy Exchange*, Policy Exchange. Retrieved from: policyexchange.org.uk/wp-content/uploads/2016/09/knowledge-and-the-curriculum.pdf (accessed: 07/12/23)

Press Association. (2015) 'Hate crimes against Muslims soar in London', *The Guardian*. Retrieved from: www.theguardian.com/world/2015/sep/07/hate-crimes-against-muslims-soar-london-islamophobia (accessed: 07/12/23)

Quintana, M. (2010) 'bell hooks/Gloria Jean Watkins (1952-2021)', *BlackPast*. Retrieved from: www.blackpast.org/african-american-history/hooks-bell-gloria-jean-watkins-1952 (accessed: 18/03/23)

Reed, T.O. (2020) *Teach Like a Champion: the effect on student achievement, behavior, and educator perceptions* (dissertation), Trevecca Nazarene University. Retrieved from: www.proquest.com/openview/af9d340303d0f278a75bd496820eb292/1?pq-origsite=gscholar&cbl=18750&diss=y (accessed: 07/12/23)

Rights Watch UK. (2016) *Preventing Education? Human Rights and UK counter-terrorism policy in schools*. Retrieved from: www.rightsandsecurity.org/assets/downloads/preventing-education-final-to-print-3.compressed-1_.pdf (accessed: 07/12/23)

Robbins, H.M. (2018) 'How we study music: navigating the whitewash', *Media Diversified*. Retrieved from: mediadiversified.org/2018/11/23/how-we-study-music-navigating-the-whitewash (accessed: 20/05/23)

Rollock, N. & Gillborn, D. (2011) *Critical Race Theory (CRT)*, British Educational Research Association online resource. Retrieved from: www.bera.ac.uk/wp-content/uploads/2014/03/Critical-Race-Theory-CRT-.pdf (accessed: 07/12/23)

Ross, E.W. (2010) 'Exploring Taylorism and its continued influence on work and schooling' in E.E. Heilman, R. Fruja & M. Missias (eds), *Social Studies and Diversity Education: what we do and why we do it* (pp.33-37), Routledge

Said, E.W. (2003) *Orientalism: Western conceptions of the Orient*, Penguin

Sawyer, R.D. (2016) 'Desperately seeking self-reflexivity: a critique of a duoethnography about becoming a postcolonial teacher' in H. Brown, R.D. Sawyer & J. Norris (eds), *Forms of Practitioner Reflexivity: critical, conversational, and arts-based approaches* (pp.117-134), Palgrave Macmillan

Shain, F. (2011) *The New Folk Devils: Muslim boys and education in England*, Trentham Books

Shakur, A. (1987) *Assata: an autobiography*, Lawrence Hill & Co.

Shor, I. (1992) *Empowering Education: critical teaching for social change*, University of Chicago Press

Simon, R. (1987) 'Empowerment as a pedagogy of possibility', *Language Arts*, 64(4), pp.370-382

Simon, R.I. (1992) *Teaching Against the Grain: texts for a pedagogy of possibility*, Bergin & Garvey

Small, I. (2019) *The Unexpected Leader: exploring the real nature of values, authenticity and moral purpose in education*, Independent Thinking Press

Solórzano, D.G. & Yosso, T.J. (2002) 'Critical race methodology: counter-storytelling as an analytical framework for education research', *Qualitative Inquiry*, 8(1), pp.23-44

Staufenberg, J. (2021) 'The big interview: Doug Lemov', *Schools Week*. Retrieved from: schoolsweek.co.uk/the-big-interview-doug-lemov (accessed: 11/03/23)

Steinberg, S.R. (2017) 'Advancing the dialogue: naming white supremacy and patriarchy as power blocs in education' in R. Race (ed), *Advancing Multicultural Dialogues in Education* (pp.279-294), Palgrave Macmillan

Stevenson, J., Demack, S., Stiell, B., Abdi, M., Clarkson, L., Ghaffar, F. & Hassan, S. (2017) *The Social Mobility Challenges Faced by Young Muslims*, Social Mobility Commission

Taylor, F.W. (1911) *The Principles of Scientific Management*, Harper & Brothers

The Economic Times. (2017) 'Muslim job-seekers are disadvantaged in UK: government'. Retrieved from: economictimes.indiatimes.com/news/international/world-news/muslim-job-seekers-are-disadvantaged-in-uk-government/articleshow/56562756.cms (accessed: 07/10/23)

The Independent. (2016) 'Anti-terror police question schoolboy for wearing pro-Palestine badge'. Retrieved from: www.independent.co.uk/news/uk/anti-terror-police-question-schoolboy-for-wearing-pro-palestine-badge-a6873656.html (accessed: 06/12/23)

Thompson, I. (2020) 'How the white-washing of British history needs to be corrected on the national curriculum', *Left Foot Forward*. Retrieved from: leftfootforward.org/2020/06/how-the-white-washing-of-british-history-needs-to-be-corrected-on-the-national-curriculum (accessed: 20/05/23)

Tracey, K. (2018) 'Stormzy should be grateful? Tell the *Daily Mail* shut up', *Media Diversified*. Retrieved from: mediadiversified.org/2018/02/27/stormzy-should-be-grateful-tell-the-daily-mail-shut-up (accessed: 07/12/23)

Tressell, R. (2004) *The Ragged Trousered Philanthropists*, Penguin

Treuhaft-Ali, L. (2016) 'The power of pedagogy: why we shouldn't teach like champions', *Cities, Suburbs and School Choice* (blog), Yale EdStudies 240. Retrieved from: citiessuburbsschoolchoice.wordpress.com/2016/05/07/the-power-of-pedagogy-why-we-shouldnt-teach-like-champions (accessed: 07/12/23)

Turner, C. (2020) 'Pearson pulls GCSE textbook following claims that it "whitewashed" Jewish history', *The Telegraph*. Retrieved from: www.telegraph.co.uk/news/2020/01/18/pearson-pulls-gcse-textbook-following-claims-whitewashed-jewish (accessed: 20/05/23)

Uncommon Schools. (2019) *Uncommon|2021 Project Narrative*. Retrieved from: oese.ed.gov/files/2019/11/uncommonschlsPN.pdf (accessed: 05/01/24)

Valenti, K.S. (2019) *A CRT Analysis of Teach Like a Champion 2.0* (master's dissertation), Loyola University Chicago. Retrieved from: ecommons.luc.edu/cgi/viewcontent.cgi?article=5011&context=luc_theses (accessed: 07/12/23)

Wanberg, K. (2013) 'Pedagogy against the state: the ban on ethnic studies in Arizona', *Journal of Pedagogy*, 4(1), pp.15-35

Ward, H. (2018) 'Direct instruction works, says 50 years of research', *TES Magazine*. Retrieved from: www.tes.com/news/direct-instruction-works-says-50-years-research (accessed: 11/12/23)

Watt, N. (2015) 'David Cameron accuses Jeremy Corbyn of being "terrorist sympathiser"', *The Guardian*. Retrieved from: www.theguardian.com/politics/2015/dec/01/cameron-accuses-corbyn-of-being-terrorist-sympathiser (accessed: 07/12/23)

Weale, S. (2014) 'The American who wrote Britain's latest teaching bible', *The Guardian*. Retrieved from: www.theguardian.com/education/2014/oct/12/american-wrote-classroom-bible-doug-lemov (accessed: 13/03/23)

Weale, S. (2023) 'Warning over unconscious bias against working-class pupils in English schools', *The Guardian*. Retrieved from: www.theguardian.com/society/2023/oct/03/warning-unconscious-bias-working-class-pupils-schools-england (accessed: 07/10/23)

Weiler, K. (1994) 'Freire and a feminist pedagogy of difference' in P. McLaren & C. Lankshear (eds), *Politics of Liberation*, Routledge

Weston, J., Boons, M.J. & Eccarius, J.G. (1953) 'The Land and Labour League', *Bulletin of the International Institute of Social History*, 8(3), pp.191-195

Whittaker, F. (2021) 'Don't teach "contested views" on white privilege as fact, DfE tells schools', *Schools Week*. Retrieved from: schoolsweek.co.uk/dont-teach-contested-views-on-white-privilege-as-fact-dfe-tells-schools (accessed: 19/02/23)

Wiliam, D. (2017) 'Creating the schools our children need: why what we're doing right now won't help much, and what we can do instead'. Presentation delivered at Bryanston Education Summit. Retrieved from: www.dylanwiliam.org/Dylan_Wiliams_website/Presentations_files/2017-06-07%20Bryanston%20Education%20Conference.pptx (accessed: 22/07/23)